Ye Must Be Born Again

A Decree to Humanity

Ben Amen

Copyright © 2019 Ben Amen.

All rights reserved. No part of this book may be reproduced, stored, or transmitted by any means—whether auditory, graphic, mechanical, or electronic—without written permission of the author, except in the case of brief excerpts used in critical articles and reviews. Unauthorized reproduction of any part of this work is illegal and is punishable by law.

This book is a work of non-fiction. Unless otherwise noted, the author and the publisher make no explicit guarantees as to the accuracy of the information contained in this book and in some cases, names of people and places have been altered to protect their privacy.

Scripture quotations are taken from the King James Version of the Bible.

ISBN: 978-1-4834-9508-8 (sc)
ISBN: 978-1-4834-9509-5 (e)

Library of Congress Control Number: 2018914528

Because of the dynamic nature of the Internet, any web addresses or links contained in this book may have changed since publication and may no longer be valid. The views expressed in this work are solely those of the author and do not necessarily reflect the views of the publisher, and the publisher hereby disclaims any responsibility for them.

Any people depicted in stock imagery provided by Getty Images are models, and such images are being used for illustrative purposes only. Certain stock imagery © Getty Images.

Lulu Publishing Services rev. date: 03/26/2019

Soon Coming Powerful and Exclusive Christian Books by Ben Amen

1. The Rapture is Coming
2. Who is going in the Rapture?
3. The Lord Jesus is Coming
4. The Seven Seals of God is Coming
5. The Seven Trumpets of God is Coming
6. The Seven Vials of God is Coming
7. The Kingdom of God; what is it?
8. What is My Position in the Kingdom of God?
9. The Commandments of the Lord Jesus
10. Signs and Wonders; is it For Today?
11. The Christian Faith; what is it?
12. The Christian Charity; what is it?
13. The Christian Talent; what is it?
14. The Dead; where are They?
15. The Falling Away is Coming.

Dedication

This book is for every living Christian who is desirous to know the truth surrounding the Christian concept called born-again. I also dedicate it to the entire members of the Singing Band of the St. Stephen Methodist Church, Ghana, and Faustina Bentsil of the same Church whose singing and dancing splurge inspires me for being with Christians; stimulating me to write this and other Christian literature that has the potential of raising the awareness of perishing ones particularly, lukewarm Christians.

Epigraph

"And moreover I saw under the sun the place of judgment, that wickedness was there; and the place of righteousness, that iniquity was there."

Ecclesiastes 3:16.

"And as it is appointed unto men once to die, but after this the judgment"

Hebrews 9:27.

"Marvel not that I said unto thee, Ye must be born again."

John 3:7.

"But when they believed Philip preaching the things concerning the kingdom of God, and the name of Jesus Christ, they were baptized, both men and women."

Acts 8:12.

Foreword

It is a great opportunity for me to write the foreword of this book, which I see as a tool, lubricant and food to the bones and souls of those who would get copies to read. After glancing through the manuscript, I feel sad for the millions of so called Christians who have departed planet earth without becoming born-again, and the millions of alleged ones living today who are blindfolded by thousands of cult Churches that teach a false born-again or do not teach at all.

The Lord Jesus introduced the born-again concept into the religious vocabulary, and it's a decree to Christians desirous of entering into the Kingdom of God to observe every (Testament) commandments, which proceeded out from His (Lord Jesus') mouth. This constitutes what is called believe in Him and this is born-again. This simple explanation of born-again has been hijacked in meaningless long theories propounded by apostate Christians, religious quacks and charlatans.

Looking at the biblical references and the sequential manner in which the facts of this book are arranged, I admit that it is the right tool (lesson notes), the right lubricant (reference source), and the right food that every Christian need to eat (read) to become born-again. I therefore highly recommend it for use in Christian homes,

Churches and every corner that a preacher stands to preach the gospel of Christ.

Mr. Abednego Abadji
Elder
The Apostolic Church Ghana
Nii Okai-Man 1, District
Accra, Ghana.

Preface

The Word of God tells us that before one can enter into the Kingdom of God he or she must be born-again. This is the new birth. In search for the new birth however, many Christians have been persuaded to confess their sins before Catholic fathers, and bishops in a norm contrary to what the Lord Jesus directed his disciples.

Some Churches induce members to repeat series of Bible verses, fast for days, recite empty apostolic creeds and sob bitterly in prayers. After going through all such ordeals, they might think they've been born-again but scriptures prove they are not.

Satan, knowing that his time on earth is short and not wishing to suffer alone in Hellfire, has commissioned his human agents who have set up thousands of Christian Churches, which adulterate the Gospel of Christ.

He has trained pastors and ministers who prophesy lies, and preach false gospel striping Christians naked, even of the little truth left in them. Through their deceptive network and evil influence, key biblical concepts particularly, born-again upon which Christianity hinges, has been banished from the pulpit since the last few decades.

It is therefore no exaggeration to say that millions of Christians had died without becoming born-again. Regardless of their ignorance, all of them shall appear before the judgment seat of the Lord Jesus on the last resurrection.

They shall be judged and cast into hellfire for not knowing what born-again specifically entailed and for not having it. Over there, they shall regret in bitterness and in anguish, but all would be too late at that time.

This is the reason why everybody must know the truth surrounding born-again so that we can see the wickedness of these Christian quack and charlatans controlling Christendom today and avoid them completely.

Acknowledgment

I would like to thank my Christian brothers and sisters across the globe whose frequent questions and comments enabled me to come out with this all-important book on born-again. I also thank my lovely wife Doreen and Children whose patience and encouragement strengthened me in the Lord throughout the days of my research.

Special thanks also goes to Elder Abednego Abadji of the Apostolic Church Ghana. Also to be remembered is my mother Mrs. Elizabeth Koomson of Mim-Brong Ahafo, Ghana for her last words of encouragement and the powerful *Abibidwom* (Native gospel music) she sang before this book went to the publishing house.

My final thanks goes to the entire management and staff of Lulu Publishing Company particularly, Mari Andrews, Publishing Consultant, without whose assistance this publication might not have been possible. I ask the Lord's blessings for all of you and those who would help to place a copy of this book in the home of Christians living everywhere in the world.

The Lord grant you all who may read this book or may hear someone who briefs you about its details eternal life so that we can meet one day in a big glory in the Kingdom of God where we shall share our never-ending stories.

Introduction

The first most frequent question Christians asked their neighbors during the seventies and eighties after "what is your name" was, "are you born-again"? In those days, information about born-again echoed in all Church rooms and every corner where a Christian stood to spread the gospel.

Today, it's very hard to meet a Church which talks about born-again. Prosperity has taken the center stage of every Church these last days. Born-again is a Christian concept, which "die-hard" Christians regard with deep and solemn respect.

It is the main pillar upon which Christianity stands and the certification for eternal life. Any Church, which doesn't teach the true born-gain, is a counterfeit one. If those who call themselves Christians were aware of this, many Churches we see today would have folded up.

In 2013, I asked two hundred Christians selected from different Christian denominations, aged between twenty and fifty years across the globe to explain what they understand by the term, born-again, and how one could be born-again.

To my surprise, ninety-nine point nine percent (99.9%) of the respondents couldn't answer me correctly at the Bible's perspective. Meanwhile, they were all active members of a Church. Is this not shocking?

I also contacted over a hundred people including pastors and Church elders from twenty countries and asked them the same question. The answers I received were so baffling. Almost all of them were deviating from the main concept of "Born-again".

A year later, I set out to visit different Christian gatherings and Churches in Ghana. To my dismay, I realized that the concept is completely phased out from the pulpit. I began to realize that Christianity is facing the biggest challenge ever.

This clearly shows that majority of people, who claim to be Christians, do not know the key concept and corner pillar upon which their own religion stands. These are the very people who claim they live their lives according to the principles and values taught by the Lord Jesus Christ.

If in these last days, pastors, Church elders, and the bulk of Christians do not know what born-again is and how one could become born-again, then it implies that the enemy has sown tares among the wheat, Matthew 13:25, and that we must be careful where we worship.

This book is specially and carefully written to clear all ambiguities and to explain born-again the same way as the Lord Jesus Christ did to his disciples. It unveils the conspiracy that has shrouded this concept for several decades and directs Christians how to become born-again in order to enter into the Kingdom of God.

It is up to you up there who profess to be Christians to lower your shoulders by discarding every little information you already have about this concept before reading this book so that the truth can set you free.

1

SATAN IS MAN'S BITTEREST ENEMY

We're living in a world where virtually every truth about creation has been hidden from the children of the one true God. Meanwhile, we have prophets, apostles, bishops and self-styled men of God who claim to be Christian "gurus" and think tanks.

Some of them perform signs and wonders, and tell us about their false dream journeys to Heaven where they've met and have had conversations with the Lord Jesus and God. However, nobody ever thought of tapping solutions to the overwhelming problems compounding our existence as the most civilized species.

As I see Christianity today, every denomination has its own views on salvation, life after death, eternal life, the Kingdom of God, and several other Christian concepts, programs and agenda that are relevant to the Church and Christian growth.

This has left many Christians in suspense because; they cannot lay hands on a single fact encircling most of these key biblical concepts and points. The truth is one, and the only place to find it is in the

Holy Bible. Sad enough, it's the same Bible wherever you go, but the message is always different.

According to the Bible, every human born to this earth is journeying through life to a final destination in eternity called the Kingdom of God where we are supposed to live forever. Those who falter on the way shall enter into eternal condemnation in hellfire.

According to the Bible, getting the Kingdom of God in eternity depends upon one's relationship with the Lord Jesus. On the other hand, going to Hell also depends upon one's relationship with the same Lord Jesus.

Every Christian would want to continue his or her existence in the Kingdom of God. Unfortunately, human's bitterest enemy, Satan, does not want this dream to come true. He embarked upon a coup d'état in Heaven with the idea of overthrowing God and taking His seat.

If he had succeeded, he would have wiped out the entire human race and thwarted all God's purposes and His good plans for humanity. However, he was overpowered by the host of angels in Heaven and was cast down to this earth to forfeit all his goodly things over there.

Because Satan has no power to fight back in reclaiming his former residence, and for lack of power to create his own world, he is now living in the universe, in caves, in valleys, in rivers, in lakes, in the sea, in the jungle, etc., on planet earth.

Guess the position, the power, the respect, and all the comforts and pleasure Satan once enjoyed as the boss of the host of heavenly angels, and imagine his condition today in the jungle on earth. He looks sad, frustrated and confused.

He has fallen from angelic grace to a beastly snake that eats rotten foods, and drinks alcoholic beverages poured on the ground. This's disgrace and big degradation! He's always depicted with ugly clothes and stinking body. He's been induced to nothing by the Lord's angels and has been tainted beyond disgrace.

The Word of God makes us to understand that the Lord God Has plans for humans, that is, to give us a final rest in the Kingdom of God after life on earth is no more, which obviously is the expectation of every Christian.

Satan, in his confused state has been doing everything he can to prevent this plan from coming through, by tempting, frustrating, persuading and deceiving Christians. He has wasted all his chances with the Lord God and has no pardon whatsoever from him.

For his punishment, the Lord God is determined to dump him into hellfire after six thousand years of his dominion over planet earth and humanity. Instead, for him to regret in sorrow and in constant pleading for forgiveness, Satan is still determined to be like the Lord God. For this reason, he has no pardon.

Satan knows that the time for his arrest, sentencing and punishment in hellfire has drawn closer. For this reason, He's now on a high alert than ever to deceive humanity. He wants humanity to be like him who has forfeited all his glories.

He's more determined to prevent as many people as he can lay hands on from entering into this blissful future kingdom of God's elect. His best strategy has been to use humans as his agents who he commissions to set up false Christian Churches that teach false gospel.

These false gospel teachers are well trained and so cunning that without the power of God and deep Bible research, one might refer them as true ministers of the Lord. They pretend as if they are angels of light, but inwardly are devils. The scripture exposed them in the days of the Lord's apostles:

> "And no marvel; for Satan himself is transformed into an angel of light. Therefore it is no great thing if his ministers also be transformed as the ministers of righteousness; whose end shall be according to their works."
>
> 2 Corinthians 11:14–15.

All over the world, you see different Christian denominations all proclaiming the message of Jesus and using the Bible as their holy book, but if you get closer to their doctrines, beliefs and norms, you will realize that they are bidding for Satan.

Meanwhile these churches are the very ones that teach born-again, the only concept that a believer must know and put to practice in order to enter into the Kingdom of God. We must all agree to the fact that Satan is humans' bitterest enemy who will never show us the right way to peace and prosperity.

Satan has managed, through these cult Churches, to explain away this all-important concept and banished every necessary information about it from the pulpit. The cover-up has increased to the extent that no one ever hears about born-again in the Church room again these last days.

Millions are dying without being born again, and very soon, it shall be your turn to go. Nevertheless, don't forget that it shall be the most saddest experience for you, your partner, relative or good friend to depart planet earth without becoming born again.

If you agree with me, then you are supposed to sit up and look for the truth. This is the time to act and to act wisely and quickly by embracing the truthful information disclosed in this book, which is a thorough Bible research work guided by the Comforter.

The Kingdom of God truly exists, but these false angels of light have dwindled the light on it making so many Christians live as if the biblical information about this kingdom were a myth. Why this wickedness?

I have personally witnessed on TV program, the president of a popular Christian denomination who openly declared that the Kingdom of God is the blessings and peace one enjoys on earth in this human existence if he or she leads a good moral life. Such an apostasy!

If this is what the president of a popular Christian denomination is saying about the Kingdom of God, what do you think would motivate the entire members to live for the Lord Jesus or to look for entry requirements into the Kingdom of God?

If you, as a Christian, were to know what the Kingdom of God is, the magnitude of peace and security, and the depth of happiness and contentment in that place, you would have given up attending these fake Churches and would have decided on what to do fruitfully with your soul.

Every man shall die, but life doesn't end in the grave. Sincere Christians who became born-again take "rest" after death, whilst recalcitrant folks who refused to become born-again do not take this "rest."

This is the main reason why this very book you are reading is topical amongst all Christian books ever written. It unveils all the secret information about the born-again concept, which has been concealed for decades.

One advice I'd like to give to the reader is that disclosure of any detailed information about born-again shall be meaningless and misleading unless I first unveil the misconception surrounding it and where one goes immediately after death.

Just like the conspiracies surrounding the flat earth and its static nature; the myth said about the distance of the sun and moon from the earth and so on; there is another vast school of conspiracy surrounding the issues bothering life after death.

Some Churches teach that sincere Christians continue their existence after death, so there is something they must do to get a better place to stay in eternity. As to where and how they take, this rest remains a riddle. Other Churches assert that when a man dies, he's left in the grave until the last resurrection.

Some of the cult Churches also teach that after death, those who did good or bad are taken to live on one of the numerous galaxies and stars in the universe. I wonder who told them there were galaxies, planets or stars existing in outer space.

I must truly tell you that everything concerning the creation of God is perfectly recorded in the Bible. The existence of galaxies, planets and stars are false theories propounded by our captors and educators who have brainwashed the whole world into thinking that these bodies exist.

Secret Spiritual societies made up of the Lodges and Freemasons have their own views. They claim that if a person dies, he or she is dead forever. In view of this, they have adopted a popular motto; "Do art thou wilt," which means that everybody must enjoy his or her rights because when one dies, he or she is dead forever.

All these groups together with the secret spiritual societies have strong points to support their claims. The fact is that all those who hold to such claims are liars and are of their father Satan who was a liar from the beginning. The question is:

- ❖ Do humans continue their existence after death?
- ❖ Is there life after death?
- ❖ Where does one go immediately after death?

2

THE DEAD; WHERE ARE THEY?

Sincere Christians believe that there is life after death. We don't need books to tell us where those who die in the Lord Jesus go after death. We need neither any sham apostle, prophet nor self-acclaimed man of God to tell us. The Bible has given us an explicit information about this.

We are all bound to die. It doesn't matter whether you are a pastor, an apostle or Pope. No matter which religion you claim to belong to and the quantum of your wealth, power, academic credentials or influence, we shall all die one day.

After death, no one has the power to talk, move, or do anything in the grave. Over there, no matter what power you had on earth, you have no control over your life. You don't tell the Lord's angels where you want to stay or what you want to do.

Whether you were a president, a top business executive, a spiritual guru, a powerful televangelist, a modern-day prophet or self-styled apostle, the angels of God don't care. They treat you according to the "believe," respect and obedience you had for the Lord Jesus whilst living on earth.

As soon as a Christian believer dies and is buried, he or she is taken to another place for rest. The remaining dead ones who did not "believe" in the Lord Jesus are also hurled to a different place; where they are kept permanently to wait for the second resurrection.

During the second coming of the Lord Jesus, true Christian believers shall resurrect. This is the first resurrection. Christian believers who'd be alive at that time together with the resurrected ones, would be given permanent and indelible bodies and we shall all be lifted from this earth to meet the Lord Jesus in the air.

After being lifted up, we shall be taken away to live in the City of the Lord Jesus in the majestic Kingdom of Heaven. The Lord Jesus told us:

> "In my Father's house are many mansions: if it were not so, I would have told you. I go to prepare a place for you. And if I go and prepare a place for you, I will come again, and receive you unto myself; that where I am, there ye may be also."
>
> John 14:2–3.

Over there, we shall continue to live with the Lord Jesus until the "Seven Seals of God, the Seven Trumpets of God and the Seven vials of God," the end time apocalyptic programs popularly called the great tribulation, which involves the complete destruction of everything on earth including all sinners, have ended.

After the destruction, the Bible tells us that the earth shall be made anew and the Saints of the Lord Jesus shall return to this earth. The refurbished earth is what the Bible calls, "The Kingdom of God."

We shall then live with the lord Jesus in the Kingdom of God for a thousand year period.

The Christians, who shall live in the Kingdom of God, shall be those who had a chance in the first resurrection. The Word of God tells us that all those who would get the chance in the first resurrection are blessed:

> "Blessed and holy is he that hath part in the first resurrection: on such the second death hath no power, but they shall be priests of God and of Christ, and shall reign with him a thousand years."
>
> Revelation 20: 6.

Then comes the souls of those who did not "believe" the Lord Jesus. They are kept in a dangerous place to wait for the final judgment day. They shall be judged according to the evil done and later dumped into an eternal hell fire to burn forever.

These two types of resurrection is what the Bible calls "the resurrection of the just and unjust. (Acts 24:15). The first resurrection, "the resurrection of the just" is for born-again Christians, and the second, "the resurrection of the unjust" is for all those who did not become born-again.

The prophet Daniel foretold us about this resurrection:

> "And at that time shall Michael stand up, the great prince which standeth for the children of thy people: and there shall be a time of trouble, such as never was since there was a nation even to that

same time: and at that time thy people shall be delivered, every one that shall be found written in the book."

"And many of them that sleep in the dust of the earth shall awake, some to everlasting life, and some to shame and everlasting contempt. And they that be wise shall shine as the brightness of the firmament; and they that turn many to righteousness as the stars for ever and ever."

Daniel 12:1–3.

Those to enter into shame and everlasting contempt include all the members of mainstream religions, the Secret spiritual societies, and idol worshippers who don't know the Lord Jesus and don't want to become born-again. The rest are lukewarm Christians who though attend Churches, but are not born-again.

In eternity, as sincere Christians would be enjoying the millennium reign in a blissful life with the Lord Jesus in the Kingdom of God, these hooligans shall remain in their tight and dangerous corners. The Bible tells us more about this:

"But the rest of the dead lived not again until the thousand years were finished."

Revelation 20: 5.

"The rest of the dead" are the wicked folks I have described above. They shall be thrown into the lake of fire after the final judgment. The Bible tells us more:

> And death and hell were cast into the lake of fire. This is the second death. And whosoever was not found written in the book of life was cast into the lake of fire.
>
> Revelation 20:14–15.

The question now is, where will the dead in the Lord Jesus be kept until the Lord organizes the first resurrection. This question has become a puzzle until this day. I am coming to unveil the mystery hidden in the Bible concerning this to settle the noisome lies cult groups, particularly, the Jehovah witnesses make on this issue.

According to this cult sect, when a person dies, he or she is dead forever. First, let's glance through the popular scripture which the Jehovah Witness quote to mislead people. We take our reading from Ecclesiastes 9:5–10.

> Ecclesiastes 9 Verse 5: "For the living know that they shall die: but the dead know not anything, neither have they any more a reward; for the memory of them is forgotten."

Let's take the passage, phrase by phrase. "But the dead know not anything." This means that the dead person does not know anything going on in the earth. The passage does not tell us they do not know what is going on at the place they are found in eternity.

"*Neither have they any more a reward.*" Note very well that the scripture did not tell us the dead has no reward in eternity. The statement is clear and true that a dead person has no reward as in wages, in salaries, in achievements, in titles or in praises on earth again.

"For the memory of them is forgotten." This obviously means that when a person dies, his or her loved ones lose memory of them. Simply put, people forget them. You can see that no phrase from this scripture talks about life in the grave, but rather, how the living man sees the dead.

> Chapter 9 Verse 6: "Also their love, and their hatred, and their envy, is now perished; neither have they any more a portion for ever in any thing that is done under the sun."

When a man dies, he doesn't know anybody in the grave to hate, and he doesn't see anything to envy. The scripture is therefore talking about a dead man's instincts whilst on earth not in the grave. To prove this let's take the second part of the scripture again:

"Neither have they any more a portion for ever in any thing that is done under the sun."

Having a portion in anything done under the sun refers to activities that people do in broad daylight whilst living. The dead person does not do anything again under the sun.

It is the work of Linguists to interpret Kings Speeches. When the wise talks, the foolish does not interpret. When the Bible speaks, the apostate Christians must keep silent. To interpret the Bible, one needs the wisdom of God not accreditation in English language or academic credentials.

The above passage we have just discussed has nothing to do with the activities that goes on in the grave, and can never be the proof that when a person dies, he or she is dead forever. This is the proof that the Jehovah Witness is a special cult Church established to distort the Bible.

I am now coming to the verses, which the "foolish" should not dare attempt to interpret:

> Ecclesiastes Chapter 9 Verse 7: "Go thy way, eat thy bread with joy, and drink thy wine with a merry heart; for God now accepteth thy works."

According to this scripture, anyone who obeys God is acceptable to Him, and such a person must eat and drink with joy because he or she has fulfilled his or her obligation as a human on earth. Man's obligation on earth therefore is to honor God his creator.

From the coming of the Lord Jesus all those who want to honor God, must do so by honoring the Lord Jesus. The Lord Jesus revealed this:

> "That all men should honour the Son, even as they honour the Father. He that honoureth not the Son honoureth not the Father which hath sent him."

> John 5: 23.

If you are someone who does not honor the Lord Jesus, then you do not obey God. This takes us to the continuation of our scripture passage:

> Ecclesiastes Chapter 9 Verse: 8 "Let thy garments be always white; and let thy head lack no ointment."

"Let thy garments be always white," does not mean that you should wear a white gown and suit every day, and "Let thy head lack no ointment" does not also mean that you should always put ointment in your head even when going to bed.

What the above scripture means is that it's appointed unto men to die one day, and once everybody shall give account of his or her deeds, we must lead a clean life devoid of anything that will make us disgustingly dirty before the lord.

In sum, the Word of God is telling us to lead an exemplary clean life devoid of sin because there is death. The Word of God wants to ask whether sleeping with your wife is all the joy one needs in this life:

> Ecclesiastes Chapter 9 Verse 9: "Live joyfully with the wife whom thou lovest all the days of the life of thy vanity, which he hath given thee under the sun, all the days of thy vanity: for that is thy portion in this life, and in thy labour which thou takest under the sun."

The WordWeb dictionary defines vanity as; "the quality of being valueless or futile." With this in mind, let's come to the actual scripture quote. To "live joyfully with the wife whom thou lovest all the days of the life of thy vanity," is not a command from Solomon for men to go and sleep with their wives for enjoyment as most of you think.

The passage says, we sleep with our wives thinking that we are enjoying the best pleasure ever, but instead we may be enjoying vanity. In the wisest sense, we need to invest our love and delight in the Lord God more than we invest in our wives, which we consider man's highest pleasure on earth.

We must work for the Lord God. This is every man's duty on earth. This is the way to please him throughout our lives until death knocks at our doors. The work we do for the Lord determines whether we shall go to Him or to Hell after death. The scripture explains it better this way:

> Ecclesiastes Chapter 9 Verse 10: "Whatsoever thy hand findeth to do, do it with thy might; for there is no work, nor device, nor knowledge, nor wisdom, in the grave, whither thou goest."

"Whatsoever thy hand findeth to do," means to do the Work of God. This is the only most important obligation for man before you consider your carpenter, teacher, piloting, nursing, etc.

"Do it with thy might," also means you should do the work with all your strength, your soul and heart in such a way that when it comes to dying for the Lord, you could die without complaining.

"For there is no work" *(*you can't serve God*)*, "nor device" (There are no musical instruments to praise Him), "nor knowledge" *(*No one will impact knowledge about God to you*)*, "nor wisdom" (There is no Word of God to study*)*, in the grave when one dies.

This is the scripture passage that the Jehovah Witness has misconstrued to mean that the dead does not live again whereas there is nothing of that sort in the scripture above. King Solomon is the writer of the book of Ecclesiastes. He was considered the wisest man of his time.

King Solomon could be ungodly contrary to the Bible's viewpoint if he had written the scripture we just read above to mean that there is no life after death. To prove that he never said anything like that listen to what he said later in the same book:

> "— because man goeth to his long home, and the mourners go about the streets. Then shall the dust return to the earth as it was: and the spirit shall return unto God who gave it.
>
> Ecclesiastes 12:5, 7.

This scripture quote tells us truthfully that King Solomon knew very well that there is life after death. According to the above scripture, when a person dies, the body rots away, but the spirit does not die or rot. It returns to God.

Having exposed the deception of the Jehovah Witness about this subject, there is no need to continue with dead assertions of other religions and cult groups. Let's quickly see where the dead goes after death.

There is a rest decreed by the Lord Jesus upon all those who die being born-again. The Bible hints us about this rest.

> "For we which have believed do enter into rest, as he said, As I have sworn in my wrath, if they shall enter into my rest: although the works were finished from the foundation of the world."
>
> Hebrews 4: 3.

The Oxford English Dictionary defines rest as:

- ❖ Cease work or movement in order to relax or recover strength.
- ❖ Allow to be inactive in order to regain or save strength or energy.

From the above two definitions, I can say that the moment one dies, whether Christian or non-Christian, the person has ceased from all works on earth. According to the scripture above, Christians do enter into rest. To enter into rest is not to remain in the grave, but to enter into a place of peace, comfort and enjoyment for the soul.

When we die as born-again children, we shall work no more to please God, but take a final rest to accomplish God's plan for humanity. Allow the Word of God to talk:

> "There remaineth therefore a rest to the people of God. For he that is entered into his rest, he also hath ceased from his own works, as God did from his."
>
> Hebrews 4: 9–10.

According to the scripture above, God, our creator also worked for six days and rested on the seventh day, and is still resting. In the same way, Christians who "believe" in the Lord Jesus and gets this rest, receives it forever.

This particular rest is enjoyed in a special place called Paradise. The Lord Jesus hinted us about paradise right at the point of death when he was on the cross:

"To day shalt thou be with me in paradise."

Luke 23: 43.

The Word of God strongly advises everyone living on earth to struggle in order to enter into this rest:

> "Let us labor therefore to enter into that rest, lest any man fall after the same example of unbelief."

Hebrews 4: 11.

The Bible says we should "labor therefore to enter into that rest" (Paradise) after death. The scripture quote above continues that "lest any man fall after the same example of unbelieve." This means that if we do not go to paradise, we go to the place where unbelievers go after death.

3

THE DEAD IN JESUS DO NOT END UP IN THE GRAVE

I have proofs from the Bible that the dead in the lord Jesus are not left to suffer in the grave, but are lifted into Paradise. In the grave, when all places are quiet and still, and whilst the dead body lies lifeless, a voice from Heaven sounds.

The voice calls out names of all those who died from earth that particular day, and those who hear their names are immediately raised up and taken to paradise. The Lord Jesus decreed this during His earthly days:

> "Verily, verily, I say unto you, He that heareth my word, and believeth on him that sent me, hath everlasting life, and shall not come into condemnation; but is passed from death unto life."
>
> John 5: 24.

The lord Jesus now shows us how the dead is raised from death (the graves) unto life (unto his rest) in paradise:

> "Verily, verily, I say unto you, the hour is coming, and now is, when the dead shall hear the voice of the Son of God: and they that hear shall live."
>
> John 5: 25.

The lord Jesus made this decree when He was on this earth. Those who will hear their names in the grave are the born-again Christians. Starting from the very day, hour and, minute the decree came out from the mouth of the Lord Jesus, all those who died born-again are raised to go to paradise.

If we believe this mystery, then there is only one thing we must do. We must ask ourselves whether we shall hear our names in the grave or shall continue to live in the place of torture prepared for those who refused to become born-again.

When a sincere Christian dies, he or she continues life in another world called Paradise. This is not the final resting place for Christians. Christians shall remain there until the glorious second coming of the Lord Jesus, which culminates the end of the world.

This is the Christian's assurance that the dead is raised:

> "And if Christ be not raised, your faith is vain; ye are yet in your sins. Then they also which are fallen asleep in Christ are perished."
>
> I Corinthians 16:17, 18.

The Lord Jesus wasn't left in the grave until the day of resurrection. He was raised after three days. When He resurrected, no one saw him openly again as before. Only His disciples and about five hundred people saw him.

In the same way, when a sincere Christian dies, the soul of the person isn't left to perish; rather, he or she is raised like the Lord Jesus. There are many instances in the New Testament where the Comforter has affirmed that the dead in the Lord Jesus aren't left in the grave, but are raised.

> "If in this life only we have hope in Christ, we are of all men most miserable."
>
> 1 Corinthians. 15: 19.

This is the reason why sincere Christian believers do not sell their souls to the devil for riches, power or fame. This is also the reason why we are not ready to visit any sham man of God for any prayers regarding prosperity or protection in life.

Whether life or dead, rain or shine, bitterness or happiness, the sincere Christian stands firm in his faith. The Word of God finally settles every argument about the gospel fact about life after death and states:

> "For if the dead rise not, then is not Christ raised:
> And if Christ be not raised, your faith is vain."
>
> 1 Corinthians 15:16–17.

The Word of God is telling us that once the Lord Jesus was raised from the dead, we shall also rise from death. However, the rest of the dead who do not hear their names in the grave are dragged to tumultuous chambers and kept securely there until the second resurrection.

According to the Word of God, they shall be judged according to their wicked deeds, and finally hurled into hellfire. The Word of God tells us:

> "And as it is appointed unto men once to die, but after this the judgment."
>
> Hebrews 9: 27.

If you believe this to be true, what manner of person are you supposed to be? You don't need to be a mere Church goer. You shouldn't be someone who knows the Bible from cover-to-cover without knowing what is born-again.

You must be born-again Christian before you can be raised from the dead to enjoy the blissful life in Paradise. Astonishingly, the happiness in paradise shall continue until we finally settle in the Kingdom of God. This is the single most important promise God has made to humanity.

Because of this promise, every Christian wants to become born-again, but the big question is how can one become born-again when Satan's cover-up is now deeper than ever these last days? Despite all the resistance from the agents of the devil, truth cannot hide forever.

4

WHAT CULT CHURCHES TEACH ABOUT BORN-AGAIN

Of late, apostate bishops and pastors running cult Christian Churches and televangelists claim that there are many gods and that humans are little gods. Sincere Christians don't believe this. We believe that there is one God, one mediator between God and men, and one Holy Bible.

> "But to us there is but one God, the Father, of whom are all things, and we in him; and one Lord Jesus Christ, by whom are all things, and we by him."
>
> 1 Corinthians 8: 6.

We also see in our world today that every Christian denomination has its own interpretation of the Bible and what born-again means to them. This is a pointer to the fact that the devil has planted its churches among the faithful ones.

Does this not also fulfil the parable of the tares where the Lord Jesus likened the Kingdom of God to a man who sowed wheat in his field?

According to the Lord Jesus, when all men went to sleep, his enemy sneaked and sowed tares among the wheat and bolted away.

When the plants grew and became ready for harvest, the servant saw the wickedness done by the enemy. The servants wondered who could have planted tares among good wheat and insisted that they go and gather them.

The Lord Jesus commissioned His apostles and disciples to set up a true Church that will direct humanity into the Kingdom of God. Satan being human's enemy, has also entered the field of Christianity and established his own Churches among the true ones.

The Lord is aware of this, but cannot take action now. The only thing He can do would be to destroy all the collaborators, but in doing so, this could affect those who might one day become saved. We find this explanation in the answer the master gave to his servants who wanted to destroy the tares:

> "But he said, Nay; lest while ye gather up the tares, ye root up also the wheat with them. Let both grow together until the harvest: and in the time of harvest I will say to the reapers, Gather ye together first the tares, and bind them in bundles to burn them: but gather the wheat into my barn."
>
> Matthew 13:29–30.

The "Tares" (False Churches and false Ministers of God) are many and uncountable, and keep on growing. Some of them say Saturday is the day to worship the Lord. Others say it is Sunday. Another group say we must be born-again. The rest say, "Jesus never asked anyone to be born-again."

The Pentecostal Churches teach that we must speak in tongues. Other Churches tell us speaking in tongues is a myth. The deception continues to grow on a long ladder leading to the creation of more and more Churches.

If you claim to be Christian with control over your own soul, and someone who can say "Yes" to what you like and "No" to what you don't like, tell me which one of them is the true Church and what does your Church say about born-again?

What the Catholic Church Say About Born-Again

The Catholic Church states that if you want to become born-again, you must be baptized by water. Therefore, the Catholics does not play with water baptism. Their belief goes on to support the fact that nothing a man does outside baptism by water is born-again.

So if you ask hundred thousand Catholics the question, "Are Catholics born again?" the answer they will give you is "Yes!" The simple reason why they will all respond in the affirmative is that all of them have been baptized with water. Is this not apostasy?

It is true that the Lord Jesus in his deliberation with Nicodemus concerning born-again mentioned water baptism, but it's not the only baptism he mentioned. He mentioned a second one that is spiritual. Where then is the second part of born-again in this Catholic dogmatic doctrine?

Why should a big Christian denomination like the Catholic do this to half the population of Christians found on the surface of the earth today? Die-hard Catholics across the globe saw this anomaly and began groaning.

The Catholic Church wouldn't have bothered if other Christian denominations had not pointed fingers at them. The Catholic Church saw the dangers ahead of their false believe and decided to do something wisely to hide this misconception from their present and future members.

The Council of Trent was called in 15th November 1551, on a peculiar date which depicts "6" "6" "6" to address the necessity for a second baptism after water baptism. This is what the Catholic Church adopted:

> "This second conversion is an uninterrupted task for the whole Church who, clasping sinners to her bosom, is at once holy and always in need of purification, and follows constantly the path of penance and renewal"

You see what the Catholics say about the second birth. Look at how deceptive they are? According to the statement above, the second birth can be done by the Church itself, which forgives members their sins, and purify them according to their own beliefs and standards.

This is not the born-again the Lord Jesus taught his disciples. The born-again Jesus taught his disciples is directly linked with salvation. According to the Lord Jesus if you want to be saved, you must be born-again. Contrary to this, the Catholics teaches that salvation can be obtained through eating of communion:

> "The doctrine of the Church is that Holy Communion is morally necessary for salvation"
>
> Source: New Advent The Catholic—

When the Lord Jesus is the only person who forgives sins, the Catholic Church from the Council of Trent began to forgive members their sins in a popular belief called *Sale of indulgence*. This is apostasy in its highest order. No man or Church can forgive people their sins and give them salvation?

> "For God hath not appointed us to wrath, but to obtain salvation by our Lord Jesus Christ."
>
> 1 Thessalonians 5: 9.

Christians obtain salvation only by believing in the Lord Jesus Christ. This exposes the fallacy of the Catholic Church and the reason why you should keep your distance from them if you want to enter the rest of the Lord Jesus after death.

What Jehovah Witness Say About Born-Again

The Jehovah Witness believes that the statement "Ye must be Born-again" is not a command but a necessity. Based on this, they claim that the new-birth is not necessary for all Christians, but to selective few.

The Jehovah Witness teach that only 144,000 people selected from their cult Church shall be given this new-birth to reign with the Lord Jesus in Heaven. (From Jehovah's Witnesses website, (www.jw.org).

I want to ask them! In which part of the Bible did the Lord Jesus or his apostles mention the number of people to become born-again? I wonder whether the 144,000 people they allege to become born-again includes Nicodemus.

If you look carefully at the Jehovah Witness, they catch people who have loose minds and adulterate them with their evil doctrines. They normally start with their deceptive literatures called "Awake" and the "Watchtower" together with numerous study materials, which they offer freely.

When you allow them to teach you, they won't give you a small gab to think or make your personal research. Before you realize, they have made you a staunch member. One thing we must remember is that the Lord Jesus never mentioned Jehovah once in His ministry, neither did His disciples.

Furthermore, the Lord Jesus never asked any of his disciples to go and evangelize in the name of any "Jehovah." If so, which Jehovah are they witnessing for? The Lord gave His disciples specific commandments concerning evangelism, which is recorded in the book of Matthew:

> "Go ye therefore, and teach all nations, baptizing them in the name of the Father, and of the Son, and of the Holy Ghost: Teaching them to observe all things whatsoever I have commanded you: and, lo, I am with you alway, even unto the end of the world. Amen."
>
> Matthew 28:19–20.

In the above scripture, no mention of any Jehovah was made here. The scripture tells us to witness for God the Father, God the Son and God the Holy Ghost. Therefore, Jehovah Witnesses are not Christians.

Jehovah Witness is a Christian cult group that has extracted some Old Testament beliefs, attached them to commandments of men to deceive people. The Word of God has this to say about the Jehovah witness:

> "This know also, that in the last days perilous times shall come. For men shall be lovers of their own selves, covetous, boasters, proud, blasphemers, disobedient to parents, unthankful, unholy, Having a form of godliness, but denying the power thereof: from such turn away."
>
> 2 Timothy 3:1, 2, 5.

The Word of God predicted that the Jehovah Witness should come in the last days. Truly, this Christian cult Church started in 1870 to fulfil its coming in the last days. We find them today to be "Lovers of their own selves." If you are not their member, they will never share their love and secret with you.

They are "covetous, boasters, proud," because if you meet the Jehovah witness, they will steal your soul into their cult group. They will then "boast" as if they are true Christians. Finally, they are "proud" of holding their adulterated Bible called the New World Translation.

They are "blasphemers," because they don't respect Jesus who says we should honor him the same way we honor God. (John 5:23)

They are "disobedient to parents, and unthankful" to the Lord God for rejecting the core message of a mediator sent by God to teach us the truth so that by believing in him, we can be saved.

They are "unholy," because whereas the Bible says drunkards shall go to hell, Jehovah Witnesses drink alcohol and teach everyone to do the same.

They, "Having a form of godliness, but denying the power thereof" appropriately befits them because they defy all the several quotations that depicts the Lord Jesus as one of the Godhead and ascribe him to an Angel.

The scripture above tells us; "from such turn away," meaning that God does not recognize them. Therefore, if you refuse to heed to the instruction of the Bible and follow this dangerous cult Church, you do so at your own risk.

The Bible continues with the verse six of 2 Timothy 3 to give us the full proof that the passage relates directly to the Jehovah witness, but not any other Christian denomination:

> "For of this sort are they which creep into houses, and lead captive silly women laden with sins, led away with divers lusts, Ever learning, and never able to come to the knowledge of the truth."
>
> 2 Timothy 3:6–7.

Truly, the Jehovah Witness creep into people's homes and claim they are evangelizing. Through this, they make captives of weak-minded people (both women and men) which the Bible call "Silly women."

Finally, you see them "ever learning, and never able to come to the knowledge of the truth." Meaning that upon all what they claim to be learning in their kingdom halls, they are unable to discern the truth and the times in which we are.

If you are a member of this Christian cult group, how can you understand what is born-again when you are everyday bombarded with fables and adulterated Christian concepts. This is the reason why you should be wide-awake so that you do not fall prey to any Christian cult group like the Jehovah witness these last days.

Some Christian denominations teach that one needs to repent; be baptized with water; fast for days; take special prayers; drink communion, count the rosary; or recite some special creed before the new-birth can take place.

Other Christian denominations think one needs to repent of his sins and practice righteous life before he or she can be born-again. Some will ask new Christian converts to continue repeating the name "Jesus" several times until they can feel the touch of the Holy Spirit.

When the said Holy Spirit (not the true one from the Lord) comes upon such members, they expect them to scream, shout, roll on the floor, bark like dogs, make unusual sounds, shiver as if they were mad, and do all sorts of actions unusual with true Christian norms.

Pentecostal Churches say that except a pastor or a man of God prays for you, and not until you are able to speak in tongues, you cannot receive the new-birth. Others will tell you to pray unceasingly for hours every day before you can get the new-birth. All these are suicidal statements to come out from the pulpit.

I read an article about born-again posted on the website by an elderly person, which argues that no one can be born-again whilst in this life except after death. He wrongly quotes from the scripture just to deceive Christians who are not ready for the truth.

There are so many different interpretations of born-again which different Christian denominations have adopted that space would not allow me to talk about in this book. If you hear some of them, your ears will tingle while others will let you fight in defense of the truth.

All these assertions by the various Christian denominations are bunch of satanic lies based upon human traditions and ridiculous manipulation of the Word of God. They are planned to lure pity and innocent souls into hellfire.

I pity ignorant and dumb followers who are turned into sheep to such great deceptions. There is no chapter in the Bible where such allegories are recorded. The wonderful aspects of such lies are that these Christian denominations wrongly quote certain portions of scripture to support their created improbable account.

I see this as tragic and disreputable hoax being perpetrated on people. (1Timothy 1:3, 4). There is only one Bible; one concept; but different interpretations. Why is this so? This is the work of Satan. I know you are a Christian seeking for the rightful information about born-again. This is coming soon.

These Practices are Not Born-Again

Eternal life comes only after a Christian has become born-again, and born-again can also come when the person has "believed" in the

Lord Jesus. Any Christian denomination, which teaches otherwise, is a cult Church and a liar. It doesn't matter whether the Church is a popular one or has existed for decades.

This implies that everlasting life is not by Peter, Paul, Mary, the Pope or any man. It is neither by Church attendance nor by one's commitment to his or her Church. It is not loyalty to pastors, prophets, apostles and offering of big donations to them.

It is not by water baptism in rivers, sprinkling of water upon new converts. It is not the quantum of tithe one pays to the Church. It's neither by ones forty days fasting nor seven days dry fasting, which normally lead victims to stomach ulcer.

Being born-again is not lengthy and noisome prayers, or cleaning Church premises, chairs and tables or washing of communion bowls. It is not being a Chorister, choirmaster, a pastor, or a deacon.

It is not by sprinkling of holy water, smearing of anointing oil or any "back to sender" oil. It is not by keeping the Saturday Sabbath or keeping the Mosaic Law. It is not by penance, confession of sins, Catechism; mass or counting of rosary.

It is not by kissing of cross, kissing the palm of a holy father, or the Pope. It is not by Purgatory or pilgrimage to any holy land. It is not by silence and meditation, burning incense; astral projection, or regular chanting of mantras.

You can read the whole Bible several times a year, fast, and pray as you read, but cannot become born-again if you do not look for the true meaning of the born-again concept and follow it accordingly.

According to the Bible, getting everlasting life is a different thing altogether. It's being saved from "death" to "life," which process is facilitated by the new-birth and this is what the Lord Jesus calls born-again.

5

DICTIONARIES AND ENCYCLOPEDIAS HAVE EXPLAINED AWAY BORN-AGAIN

The Chambers 21st Century Dictionary explains born-again as "someone filled with a new spiritual life converted or re-converted, especially to a fundamentalist or evangelical Christian faith." Let's digest this definition.

This definition of born-again is trying to convince Christians that when we see someone behaving strangely in the Church during prayers or hours of ministration, we should accept this person as having been born-again.

This is not the true meaning of born-again? This interpretation does not make one sense to the true Christian believer who knows exactly what born-again is.

The Wordweb Dictionary defines born-again as "Spiritually reborn or having changed religion." This is another shocking definition of the concept. What type of spiritual birth are the authors of this dictionary talking about?

If the Freemason, the Shinto, Buddhist or Hindu is spiritually born or have changed religion, does this have any link with what born-again means to the Christian? This definition seems to ridicule Christians and it's a blatant lie.

The Macmillan English Dictionary for Advanced Learners also defines "a born-again Christian as someone who has had a strong religious experience and is therefore very enthusiastic about their people." How good does this sound in your ears? Does it make any meaning to you as a Christian?

The second meaning given by this same dictionary states that "a born-again person is someone enthusiastic about a belief or ways of life that is new to you or has recently become involved with again."

Primarily, one does not need any kind of religious experience before the person can be born-gain. The Buddhist, the Hare Krishna, Yogi or members of the mainstream religions do not need any religious experience in order to become born-again? Born-again is not the concept of any of these religions? Born again is a Christian concept and have relevance for only Christians.

Furthermore, what kind of enthusiasm are the authors of the Macmillan dictionary talking about? The Lord Jesus did not ask anybody to become enthusiastic with any religious belief before he or she can become born-again.

In addition, He never mentioned any word like "belief" when he was teaching Nicodemus the concept of born-again. Why are people forcing to interpret such an important concept in a way contrary to what the Lord taught his disciples?

One would ask if the authors of these dictionaries didn't read the Bible before concluding on what they claim are the interpretation of the concept. This is the true picture of massive misconception surrounding the born-again concept.

Christians seeking to know what born-again means consult these dictionaries and are carried away in understanding for life. Those who turn to their pastors for explanation, get the same wrong signals leaving virtually every Christian who walks on planet earth today in the dark about the true born-again concept.

I asked a popular pastor friend how one can become born-again. He looked at my face sternly and smiled. He answered that anyone who believes in the Lord Jesus was born again. This is quite true and a good answer I never expected from him.

I then asked him what it is to "believe" in the Lord Jesus. On hearing this, he burst out laughing again and asked if I do not know what it is to "believe" in Jesus. I persuaded him to tell me what he knows and to my dismay, he was telling me about trust in Jesus who answers prayers, and can do everything one needs.

I also smiled back at his answer and told him that was a bit dicey. To believe Jesus is not to trust him or hope in him. Looking deeply into how people understand this all-important Christian concept, there is a worth of evidence that there exists a conspiracy somewhere to define away the true born-again concept.

The definitions given by these dictionaries as well as countless articles and books written by Christian think tanks, and pastors on born-again, portray a sinister and crafty plot by an organized group somewhere, since time immemorial to destroy Christianity.

How can one understand born-again, and how can the person know which procedures to pass in order to become born-again when renowned dictionaries are not only trying to explain the term in the English language, but are also trying to hide its true meaning from the general public?

Why are the dictionaries not giving one explanation of born-again, but each going a different direction? This is the reason why we must take this book on born-again very serious. The reason is that you can visit all libraries or surf the internet, but can never know what is born-again and how one can become born-again.

By the Word of God, I am coming to teach you what born-again is. This isn't what you already know. It's also not what you've read about in Christian cult books. This is the born-again that the Lord Jesus himself taught his disciples, and this is the one He commands you and I as well as every Christian to believe in order to get eternal life.

If you claim you love the Lord Jesus and you're interested to know the truth, this is the opportune time for you. Sit comfortably in your seat and let the Lord Jesus teach you.

6

WHAT IS BORN-AGAIN?

Born-again is eternal life, and eternal life is born-again. The two are intertwined, and because of their symbiotic nature, no one can separate them. These two concepts are directly linked with entry into the Kingdom of God.

Born-again is believe in the Lord Jesus Christ that He is the only begotten son of God, and the second person of the Holy Trinity who can forgive sins. It is also the believe in the Lord Jesus that He is the only one who grants eternal life to those seeking to enter into the Kingdom of God.

If you hear the Word of God and believe, you must agree within the heart, soul and mind that you will continue to believe this word the rest of your life. You must also agree to observe all the commandments of the Lord Jesus.

If you agree to the above, and make the slightest attempt to observe them, you have made a progressive move in Christianity; and depending upon the level of your conviction; you can receive the new-birth. However, this can only be granted at the discretion of the Lord God.

Born-again is in twofold; the first birth and the second birth.

The First Birth

When someone agrees to become a Christian, the person must agree that his previous life in the world was adulterated with sins, which the Lord Jesus abhors. The person must therefore agree that it's only the Lord Jesus who can pardon him or her of these sins.

Upon this conviction, the person agrees that he or she won't go back to sin again. This is followed by the actual baptism, which is done in a river or stream. This alone counts nothing unless it's linked with the spirit baptism (The Second Birth)

The Second Birth

This comes about when the person who expresses the desire for eternal life entrust his or her deep believe in the Lord Jesus Christ that He's the second person of the Holy Trinity; and that He's also God.

The person then develops great interest in the Lord Jesus Christ, believe in Him, and begins to observe all His commandments. As he does these things, he or she sets on the way to becoming spiritually born-again. Depending upon the person's conviction and level of believe, the Lord grants this person the spiritual-birth.

It can take less than an hour to believe deeply in the Lord Jesus and to receive the second birth. It can also take a person his or her whole lifetime as a Christian, but may not get the second birth. It all depends upon the Church you attend and the type of gospel you study.

In sum, born-again is believe in the Lord Jesus Christ; a self-commitment to stop sinning, and a promise within one's soul, heart and mind to observe all the commandments of the Lord Jesus and to follow Him the rest of one's life with the sole aim of getting eternal life. When at the discretion of the Lord God this believe is genuine, the Lord Jesus grants the person to become born-again.

This is the biblical definition for born-again. This is the born-again the lord Jesus wants us to teach others. Any statement outside this truth can never be considered as the truth. It may be another born-again by one of these cult Churches.

Having explained it this way, foolish Christians shall jump to the conclusion that they know what is born-again and that they are born-again, whereas they don't understand the definition and the processes involved very well.

Born-again grants one the opportunity to see and to enter into the Kingdom of God after death. If you are desirous to become born-again, you do less whilst the Lord Jesus does more. You don't have to pray to Jesus to give it to you. This is a wrong approach.

All you need to do as a Christian is to allow the Words of the Lord Jesus to increase in you, minute by minute, hour by hour and day by day. The more you commit yourself to this course; you receive the new-birth automatically.

Born-again is an entry visa into the Kingdom of God. Without it, one cannot enter there. This is the born-again the Lord Jesus himself taught his disciples, and this is what you must accept in order to get eternal life. If you believe this, you believe into eternal life, if you reject it, you reject into eternal condemnation.

With the exception of this truthful biblical explanation, you don't have to be fascinated or threatened with any lengthy or stylish meaning or explanation of born-again. From this point, I will urge you to read this definition over again, and digest it deeply in your mind before you continue to read the rest of the book.

Also, don't be enchanted by any other definition or articles from an internet bloc which has no basis in the Bible. This is the beginning of the lectures on a controversial Christian concept. When the Physics lecturer comes to class and defines "matter" to you, it doesn't mean you know everything about matter.

You need to know it's composition, characteristics, uses, etc. Therefore the definition of born-again I have given above doesn't give you the in-depth knowledge about the concept. I will come to this very soon for you to know your right from left.

7
THE LORD JESUS TEACHES THE BORN-AGAIN CONCEPT

The Lord Jesus gave Christians full details on born-again when one of the rulers of the Pharisees by name Nicodemus visited him one night commending the Lord that He is a man from God. In the conversation between the two, the Lord Jesus decreed the concept, born-again, taught the world what it is, and how one can receive it.

It is expedient to believe what the Lord Jesus tells you than to believe in a Church or a pastor whose spiritual identity you do not know. Let's read the Bible account from the book of John Chapter three (3) to know what exactly born-again is and how one can receive it.

> John Chapter 3:1-2 "There was a man of the Pharisees, named Nicodemus, a ruler of the Jews. He came to Jesus by night, and said unto him, Rabbi, we know that you are a teacher come from God: for no man can do these miracles that you do, except God be with him."

Note very carefully that Nicodemus first expressed believe in the Lord Jesus when he addressed Him as a man who "Comes from

God." He also affirmed that all the miracles by the Lord Jesus had the Lord God's backing.

Because of the distinct "believe" Nicodemus expressed in the Lord Jesus, He saw the need to disclose information about a new concept called born-again into the religious vocabulary that His followers; present and future would need to know and practice in order to enter into the Kingdom of God.

A careful study of the Bible reveals that anytime an expression of "believe" in the Lord Jesus is manifested upon meeting him face-to-face, there is the pronouncement of eternal life (born-again) in reciprocal.

Let's compare the believe that Nicodemus had in the Lord Jesus with the woman caught in prostitution. This woman never expressed "believe" in the Lord Jesus, after she had wonderfully been freed from her accusers. John 8:3–11.

Because of that no eternal life, or Kingdom of God was pronounced here. Therefore, for this new Christian concept and lesson to have come out from the Lord Jesus is because of the expression or statement of "believe" made by Nicodemus when he met the Lord one-on-one.

There are three key points in Nicodemus' statement of believe. These are:

- ❖ Jesus is the Son of the Almighty God.
- ❖ The Almighty God sent Him.
- ❖ All the mighty works He did had the backing by the Almighty God.

Once again, I tell you that these comments by Nicodemus are expressions of strong "believe" in the Lord Jesus. Nicodemus sees Jesus not as one of the common sons of God or prophets. He sees a different person altogether.

Being a scholar, a divine master of the Mosaic Law, a member of the Sanhedrin (The ruling council of the Jews), and someone well vexed in the Old Testament Bible, he had read extensively about the Lord Jesus and believes that He is the Promised Messiah fore-told by the prophets of God.

Nicodemus recollected his memories in the scriptures and remembered one good statement made about the promised messiah in the book of Malachi:

> "Behold, I will send my messenger, and he shall prepare the way before me: and the Lord, whom ye seek, shall suddenly come to his temple, even the messenger of the covenant, whom ye delight in: behold, he shall come, saith the LORD of hosts."
>
> Malachi 3:1.

According to this Bible quote, the Almighty God Himself would one day disguise Himself and dwell with men on earth. Nicodemus knew the fulfillment of this prophecy was the Lord Jesus before whom he sat to converse. He is also familiar with many other prophetic writings about Him:

> "For unto us a child is born, unto us a son is given: and the government shall be upon his shoulder: and his name shall be called Wonderful, Counselor, The

mighty God, The everlasting Father, The Prince of Peace."

Isaiah 9: 6.

According to the above Bible quote, the world must expect a human born of a woman who isn't an ordinarily human, but the Almighty God in disguise. God came down in the person of the Lord Jesus for His people to see him. Anyone who refutes this fact is the devil.

The Lord Jesus is God who left his throne in Heaven and came to earth. He only had to spend thirty-three years, which was some forty-seven minutes fifty-two seconds Heavenly time, when we go by the calculation that a thousand years is as to the Lord God one day.

Imagine thirty-three years when the son of God must pass through several agonies to teach humankind the truth about eternal life and the Kingdom of God. This was a hard task for someone by whom all things were created to have accomplished.

Notwithstanding, once the Lord God has promised His people about this visit, He must fulfill it. So, the Almighty God came to earth in the person of Jesus. This was the conviction of Nicodemus, and this is what compelled him to visit the Lord Jesus to inquire about everlasting life.

Again, Nicodemus was deeply moved with the powerful works the Lord Jesus performed in towns and villages of Israel and knew for sure that He was indeed the promised God. Notwithstanding, being a learned man seeking for the truth, he must interview him personally before confirming the fulfilment of these prophecies.

After all, how can God leave his throne for a few minutes and travel to a jungle earth because of humanity. As long as He remains on earth, who is ruling the kingdom of Heaven? He needs to understand all these riddles perfectly well so that he can be the first to teach his compatriots if he finds the Lord Jesus to be the Promised Messiah.

This compelled him to come to the Lord Jesus at such a crucial night. The Lord Jesus upon seeing such a deep believe coming from a ruling member of the Sanhedrin, did not let him finish his speech, but intervened and said:

> John Chapter 3: 3 "Verily, verily, I say unto thee, Except a man be born again, he cannot see the kingdom of God."

When the Lord Jesus was in Jerusalem at the Passover, although many people believed in his name, when they saw the miracles, which he did, yet He didn't tell them anything. Nicodemus made a follow up to the Lord's residence to inquire about the most important thing in humans' life.

The Lord knows what is in man John 2:25 and because of that before Nicodemus opened his mouth, he knew his thoughts. For sure, Nicodemus came to the Lord Jesus purposely to know about entry conditions into the Kingdom of God.

Straight away, the Lord told him, if it's the Kingdom of God for which he came, "except" he's born again." Except is a conditional word meaning that it is compulsory that one becomes born-again if he or she wants to enter into the Kingdom of God.

"Ye" in the King James Version means that Nicodemus and all other people present and future must be born-again. In simple English, the Lord Jesus said Nicodemus together with every Christian seeking to see and to enter into the Kingdom of God must be born-again.

From the above Bible quote, it is evident that born-again is the Kingdom of God, and the Kingdom of God is born-again. You can straighten bananas, but cannot straighten life, and no matter how you tame the rat, its tale would remain the same.

No matter what false Christian denominations say about the concept, the command to Christians to become born-again shall remain unalterable until the Lord's second return. The command is:

> "Except a man be born again."

This is a command statement, a commandment and a decree to humanity. In the Book of John, the Lord Jesus told us that all those who love him should keep his commandments, John 14:15. The Lord wants His followers to keep His commandments.

After His resurrection, and prior to His ascension, the Lord Jesus seriously stressed that Christians should keep His commandments, not just a few of them, but all:

> "Go ye therefore, and teach all nations, baptizing them in the name of the Father, and of the Son, and of the Holy Ghost: Teaching them to observe all things whatsoever I have commanded you"
>
> Matthew 20:19–20.

Note very well that the Lord Jesus has seriously commanded us to observe "All things." All things here, represents all the commandments that came out from his (the Lord's) mouth and those He gave us through His apostles who wrote the epistles.

Therefore, anyone who does not observe the entire commandment given by the Lord Jesus as recorded in the New Testament Bible does not love him and is not a sincere Christian. No matter what understanding such a person may claim to have about the Bible or the Lord Jesus, this person is not born-again.

One of the commandments in discussion says; "Except a man be born again." This simply put is "Ye must be Born again." If anyone loves the Lord Jesus and claim to be Christian, there is no need for any further explanation or comments. The command is "Ye must be born again."

In all his life and with his position and experience as a Pharisee; a self-righteous sectarian; and a mature practicing lawyer, the Lord Jesus says Nicodemus must be born-again. This statement seems awkward to such a man of high dignity. However, God is not respecter of persons. (Acts 10:34).

With all his PHD degrees as a divine master of the Mosaic Law, Nicodemus had never heard or come across born-again in the scriptures or in any of the numerous religious books, he had read. He started cogitating about this command statement, which kept echoing in his ears, "Except a man be born again."

He wondered whether born-again was a new concept that the Lord Jesus was introducing to the world or; it was already existent in religious books. I am sure he kept repeating this statement over, and over again in his mind until he didn't know what to say next to make his visit purposeful.

In fact, Nicodemus sees born-again as a New Hebrew vocabulary and an improbable religious theory! A new concept, giving details of how one can be permitted to "see" the Kingdom of God Nicodemus was completely lost on hearing this, so he quickly retorted:

> John Chapter 3: 4 "How can a man be born when he is old? Can he enter the second time into his mother's womb, and be born?

So many people make fun of this question and think it wasn't necessary for Nicodemus to have asked that. I tell you. It's the wisest question that has ever been asked in the history of humanity, and I don't think any wiser question can arise besides this one until the world comes to its end.

Nicodemus was contemplating whether one needs some blessings or rebirth from the biological mother in order to see the Kingdom of God. Nicodemus bears a title for asking such a sensible question which becomes an axe on the root of every soul living. What is this title, and why am I saying this?

As far as the Kingdom of God is concerned, the Word of God classifies humankind in three categories; the wise, the foolish and the greatest. Millions of people who "believe" the Lord Jesus to become born-again Christians are wise people.

Several millions who reject the truth about the Lord Jesus are the foolish ones. Finally, those who observe the commandments of the

Lord Jesus and teach others to do the same are the greatest. Read Matthew 5:19.

The twelve apostles had the invitation in a divine selection to take their great positions. It's upon their shoulders that we had the New Testament Bible; the divine constitution which makes a person greatest or wise.

They are considered the greatest men in the history of humanity and in the Kingdom of God. This is simply because they wrote the New Testament, kept it securely for future generations, and spread the gospel of the Lord Jesus.

Nicodemus was among the elite class of his days. He wasn't invited by the Lord Jesus, but in his quest for the Kingdom of God went to push the Lord Jesus to tell the world the processes through which one can pass to see the Kingdom of God.

It is through Nicodemus, that such detailed lessons on seeing and entering into the Kingdom of God came to the whole world. That's why he's also considered the wisest man that ever lived on planet earth after the coming of the Lord Jesus.

We must bear with his confused state because the answer the Lord Jesus gave him wasn't clear at all to a non-believer like him. It is the same with millions of Christians seeking for the truth about the Kingdom of God.

We must again bear with his confused state because two thousand years after asking this great question, and after two thousand years that the Lord had answered him, the bulk of Christians doesn't understand what is born-again and how one can be born-again.

Nicodemus has asked the Lord Jesus a question. He wants to know how one can be born again when the person is old. He again wants to know whether the person will re-enter his mother's womb and be given another birth. Is this not an interesting, and a wise question?

No human on earth could answer this question, because none of us knew what was born-again until the Lord Jesus had added this concept to the Christian vocabulary. When the Lord Jesus heard this question posed by Nicodemus, instead of explaining, He rather added more complications to Nicodemus' cogitation.

We all know very well that Nicodemus who sits before the Lord Jesus isn't illiterate. He's a scholar with powerful degrees. He's not an ordinary or common person who can be manipulated with words and phrases. We also know that the Lord Jesus doesn't lie or manipulate people.

The Word of God has seriously told us that every Word that proceeds out from the mouth of the Lord Jesus is Spirit and it's fire. (John 6:63). Nicodemus is also aware of the fact that it's good to obey God than man. (Romans 3:4). This is a great fusion between the Old and New Testament Bibles.

Seeing Jesus as God who sits before him, he was determined to mark Him word-by-word, phrase-by-phrase, and precept-by-precept to get what he wanted. The Lord Jesus must tell the world how a man can be born-again after the natural birth by the mother.

This type of conversation is not the type that Christians must ridicule and spread as a joke. It's not the type religious fanatics and the heathen must ignore. It's all about life and about one's entry into the

Kingdom of God. It's all about every man's eternity and a plan to escape from the danger of condemnation.

Let's see the reply the Lord Jesus gave to Nicodemus as well as the world:

> John Chapter 3:5 "Verily, verily, I say unto thee, Except a man be born of water and of the Spirit, he cannot enter into the kingdom of God."

This is another strong command; "Except a man be born of water and of the Spirit, he cannot "enter" into the kingdom of God." Christianity is made up of sets of commandments of the Lord Jesus, which every Christian is obliged to observe.

As a Christian, you must be able to say fifty of the commandments of the Lord Jesus off heart. You must know the commandment on the Kingdom of God and about the end of the world. You must know the commandments on the Lord's Day (Sunday) and many others, which you need to guide you in everyday life.

If you don't know these basic commandments, then forget it, you're doomed. How can one live a perfect Christian life without knowing the set of commandments or testaments that makes a Christian?

One day, I went to wedding and met a pastor who graced the party with a short sermon that I found irrelevant for the occasion. I approached him later and asked if he could tell me ten of the Lord's commandments on marriage so that I could answer my friends at the same table with me.

These friends wanted me to tell them some few Christian instructions on marriage. Try as he did, the answer couldn't come. Rather, the pastor asked me to tell my friends to meet him at the office for counselling on marriage.

You are not different from this pastor if you love to listen to preachers who tell stories about the Lord Jesus, His apostles, and other Bible figures, but not the commandments of the Lord Jesus.

If you are ignorant about the commandments of the Lord Jesus, then your claim as a Christian is sycophancy.

In the same vein, any pastor who doesn't know the commandments of the Lord Jesus is a poster, not pastor. If you attend their Churches, then you're all born-ago, not born-again. I don't say this to condemn anybody, but I am saying this because most Christians are not ready to study the Bible.

So many Christians including renowned ministers of popular Churches read portions of the Bible that gives them hope and happiness in this life, leaving behind the intricate part which gives eternal life.

Again, I don't say this to threaten anybody as if Christianity were such a complicated worship which requires observances that only a few people can honor; or that the Bible can be understood by only a few people.

Notwithstanding, Christianity is not that bread and butter we eat in the Church rooms every Sunday these last days. It is not listening to the prosperity gospel for only a few minutes followed by noisome music, wailing, and rolling on the floor. These things are nuisance to the Lord Jesus.

Again, Christianity is not the super-marketing and extortion of money from members that goes on during every Church service. It's neither the heavy tithe you pay nor your loyalty to the Church, its pastor and members. Christianity is observing everything the Lord Jesus commanded us.

Anything outside this is the worshipping of another Jesus in a cult Church, not the one true Jesus of the Bible. If you agree with me, then I am telling you again that there is a command from the Lord Jesus, which says that every Christian must be born of "water" and with the "Spirit." This is born-again.

It's not the born-again you already know that matters, but it's by knowing exactly what the birth by water and the birth by the Spirit is that counts. Many people know the birth by water, but in search for the Spirit's birth, they had met familiar spirits and think they have the Holy Spirit of God.

Let's come back to the conversation between the Lord Jesus and Nicodemus. We normally hear the Lord Jesus say; "Verily," Verily." In the Bible. Anytime you hear the Lord Jesus say this before any statement, it's the time He's raising a serious issue or making a decree on earth.

It is the time He's swearing by Himself to testify that whatever He is coming to say is the truth; the absolute truth, and nothing, but the truth. Anyone who swears an oath swears by a superior power higher and above him.

Jesus is the Word of the Bible, and being God on earth, He had nothing to swear with, but by himself. He therefore uses "Verily," "Verily" to prove that whatever He is coming to say is what has been decreed in the Kingdom of Heaven.

The Lord Jesus is now coming to answer Nicodemus who is a bit confused because, he now knows that we don't need to enter into our mother's womb once again before we can become born-again. The Lord has told him plainly that we must be born-again with "water' and with the "Spirit."

These are the two births, which every Christian needs in order to "see" and to "enter" into the Kingdom of God. Nicodemus, having said nothing, the Lord Jesus continued and said:

> John Chapter 3:6 "That which is born of the flesh is flesh; and that which is born of the Spirit is spirit."

The Lord Jesus has made it distinctively clear that each of the two births is different from the other. The answer is not clear at all because we don't know which type of water, gives birth to the flesh and how the Spirit gives birth to the spirit.

Nicodemus seems confused like you and me at this point for four main reasons:

- ❖ *Firstly:* He sees that it is a command from the Lord Jesus to him and the rest of humanity to become born-again if we want to "see" and to "enter" into the kingdom of God.
- ❖ *Secondly:* Nicodemus was thinking about how the "new birth" could be possible after one is born into this world.

- ❖ *Thirdly:* Getting this new birth would let one "see" and "enter" into the Kingdom of God, which are two different things altogether. He would like to know the difference between seeing and entering into the Kingdom of God.
- ❖ *Lastly:* Birth as we all know is not done in "water" and it's not done in "the spirit," but through a woman. If the Lord Jesus is introducing another way, then he would like to know how such births could take place.

You may ask why the Lord Jesus selectively used the word 'see.' and 'enter' in two different statements almost meaning the same. The fact is that you can see a city, but may not enter into it. On the other hand, the moment you enter a city, you have seen it. This calls for further explanation.

"To See the Kingdom of God"

The Lord Jesus is saying that when you receive the new birth, though you may still be living on earth, yet the secret and all relevant information about the Kingdom of God is opened to you. In the book of Mark, the Lord Jesus told us about this:

> Unto you it is given to know the mystery of the kingdom of God: but unto them that are without, all these things are done in parables."
>
> Mark 4: 11.

If you are given the mystery of the Kingdom of God, it means you have been granted to see everything in this kingdom whilst you're still living on earth. According to the Lord, it is not every Christian who is given secret information about the Kingdom of God except those who are born-again.

A friend can tell you the secret of a true story and after he or she has finished, you will tell the friend, "I see," meaning that you now know the secret of the whole story. You can't see the story with your eyes, but because you have heard the story and understands it you can say, "I see."

Only born-again Christians are given the opportunity to see (know) the mysteries surrounding the Kingdom of God. You may want to have some hints about the mystery of the Kingdom of God:

- ❖ The location of the Kingdom of God.
- ❖ Governance in the Kingdom of God.
- ❖ Angelic inventions and technology beyond human comprehension in the Kingdom of God.
- ❖ How to get a special reward or position in the Kingdom of God.
- ❖ The creativity that exists there and how Christians are going to eat, drink, enjoy and live there. Etc., etc.

There are so many secret information about the mystery of the Kingdom of God, which space and time won't allow me to talk about here. Meanwhile, no single mystery is found anywhere in any book, except in the Bible.

Take note that the born-again person does not see any visions or receive any mysteries from the Lord Jesus about the Kingdom of God except what is already written down in the Bible. Take this very serious.

If you're not careful, someone may act strangely and claim he or she's got the Holy Spirit baptism whereas this may come from some familiar spirit. For sure, infernal spirits sometimes capture images from a pit and tells you those nuisances came from the Kingdom of God.

Information about the Kingdom of God are recorded in the Holy Bible, but because you are not born again, your capacity for rationale thought about godly things is so weak to pick such information.

If you want to know mysteries of the Kingdom of God, don't just read the Bible. Read it for a purpose and the Lord will interpret everything verse-by-verse, and word-by-word to you. The entire Bible is divided into seven gospels. These are:

- ❖ The Gospel of God.
- ❖ History of Israel and the Wonders of God.
- ❖ History of the Lord Jesus and His Apostles.
- ❖ The prosperity gospel.
- ❖ The Gospel of Christ.
- ❖ The Gospel of the Mystery of the Kingdom of God, and.
- ❖ The Everlasting Gospel.

As far as I know, the early apostles preached the Gospel of Christ, and the Gospel of the Mystery of the Kingdom of God. The seventh gospel, "The everlasting Gospel," is not yet preached in the world. It shall be preached at the time when the "Mark of the beast" shall become mandatory on earth.

Our modern day Churches now preach the prosperity gospel. Everywhere you go, the message is the same. Some Christian denominations like the Seventh-day Adventist teach the gospel of God;

the history of Israel, and the wonders of God. They occasionally mix this with the history of the Lord Jesus and His Apostles.

How can one become born-again when he or she does not study the gospel of Christ? Again, how can this same person know about deeper things about God, and as well enter into the Kingdom of God when he or she does not know the mystery of the Kingdom of God.

We are in the last days so the truth must come out for everybody to know the queue he or she is following. It will be unwise to defend any Church when you have not dived deep into the scriptures to know the nefarious deeds of some of these Churches you attend.

I love everybody and wish all of you got the opportunity to enter into the Kingdom of God, which the Lord Jesus says is spacious with many mansions and better things.

Therefore, if this teaching offends you, it means you aren't defending the truth but lies. If this is so, then you aren't ready to "see" and to "enter" into the Kingdom of God. What I want to tell those of you trapped in cult Churches teaching false born-again is that it is enough!

Take a moment and search the King James Bible, and search for "the gospel of Christ," and "the mystery of the Kingdom of God," and you shall be left with no doubt about the truth I am telling you today.

The Lord Jesus says those who want to know (see) all the secret information about the final place prepared for all Christians who observe the commandments of the Lord Jesus after we die from here must be born-again.

This is what the Lord Jesus means by "Except a man be born again, he cannot see the kingdom of God." We have seen how one can "see" the Kingdom of God. Let's come to how one can "enter" into the Kingdom of God.

To "Enter Into the Kingdom of God"

The saints of the Lord Jesus shall enter into the Kingdom of God when the Lord Jesus returns for the second time in the rapture and take us to where He lives. After spending some time with Him, He will bring us back here to earth again.

This shall be the time after the Lord God has completely destroyed the earth and refurbished it. The refurbished earth is the precise location of the Kingdom of God. The moment the Saints of the Lord return from Heaven to take the refurbished earth, we have entered into the Kingdom of God.

The Lord Jesus declared, "Except a man be born of water and of the Spirit, he cannot enter into the kingdom of God." This means that some people may "see" the Kingdom of God, but shall not "enter" into it.

These people learn secret information about the kingdom of God, but because they do not know what it is to "believe" the Lord Jesus, they are not born-again. This category of people are what the Bible calls, "Lukewarm" Christians.

Before Nicodemus could alter a word, the Lord Jesus continued:

> John Chapter 3:6 "That which is born of the flesh is flesh; and that which is born of the Spirit is spirit."

Nicodemus like many other Christians need the Lord Jesus to explain further, what He actually means by "that which is born of the flesh is flesh; and that which is born of the Spirit is spirit." Knowing the intentions of Nicodemus, the Lord Jesus came down and with much patience addressed him:

> John Chapter 3:7 "Marvel not that I said unto thee,
> Ye must be born again."

The Lord Jesus is telling Nicodemus and the entire world that we must not be astonished by the command to become born-again." According to the Lord, it is a new-birth, which is compulsory for everyone who wants to see the Kingdom of God and to "enter" into it.

The Lord Jesus says we shouldn't marvel hearing this from Him. What the Lord Jesus wants to tell Nicodemus, you and the world is that humans were not sent to earth to do whatever we like. We were sent here to study how to live in the future kingdom that God has prepared for humanity who obey him.

According to the Lord Jesus, we mustn't "marvel" (challenge) this commandment which requires everybody to become born-again. You can "marvel" (challenge) this commandment if you don't want to see and to enter into the Kingdom of God.

According to the short explanation given by the Lord Jesus, born-again is in two stages: physical initiation into Christianity and a spiritual seal, which enables Christians to know all the mysteries about the kingdom of God and to enter into it.

He says this because every religion of the world has its own way of initiating its new members. The Shinto, Hindu, Muslim,

Judaism, Yoga, Confucians and virtually all mainstream religions and secret societies have their own ways of initiating new members.

Cult Churches like the Catholic, Latter-day Saints, Jehovah Witness and the rest have their own way of initiating new members. After initiation, the new convert is taking to a higher level in spirituality and training before confirmation.

The Freemason religion for instance, has its own set of rules and ways of initiating new members.

After one is accepted into it, you need to go through series of training and practices to enhance your spiritual growth. This growth process begins with a 1st degree to the 33rd degree.

We know for sure that the various initiations organized by these religious groups require commitment by the new convert and how this member can remain faithful to the religion. It is the same with Christianity.

The Lord Jesus says we should be initiated into Christianity by a process called the Water birth. This must be followed by another; the spirit birth. This is the new-birth. Nicodemus now understands it, and I am sure you also understand it now.

Nicodemus was silent because he was quite at sea on this subject. According to the Lord Jesus, He is the one introducing into the world for the first time the concept called born-again, which must become binding on everyone who becomes His follower or Christian.

The Lord Jesus Lays More Emphasis on the Spirit Birth

At this point Nicodemus was a bit settled in understanding, and I believe you are likewise settled. If so, the Lord Jesus is going further in explanation to tell us how the new process can work.

> John Chapter 3:8 "The wind blows where it wants, and you hear the sound thereof, but cannot tell where it comes from, and where it goes: so is every one that is born of the Spirit."

You can see from the above scripture quote that the Lord Jesus is going deeper in spirit. At this point, He dropped the water baptism, which is of less value to Christian growth and shifted to the Spirit baptism.

According to Him, when water baptism is being done, the person being baptized sees all the processes involved, but the Spirit birth is different. In this type of birth, the person does not become aware from where and when the Spirit birth is coming.

Again the Lord mentioned that no one can tell "where the spirit goes." This means that no minister, or prophet, or apostle, or man of God can tell when a member of his Church received the spirit-birth or became born-again.

Let's once again look at the scripture quote from this perspective. The Lord said; "The wind blows where it wants, and you hear the sound thereof, but cannot tell where it comes from." You see clearly here that there is no mention of doctrines, prayers, fasting or tongues speaking here before one can receive the Spirit birth.

Open your eyes very well to the fact that the Lord Jesus did not mention any type of work or an instance where the Spirit would be commanded by a pastor or a man of God before He comes to baptize a Christian convert.

"The Wind blows where it wants" also means that no one can command the Holy Spirit to come and baptize any new Christian convert. The Lord chooses the one who must receive the Spirit birth and who to be denied.

Therefore, any pastor who lines up hundreds of people and ask them to pray for the Spirit birth does so out of ignorance and abuse of scripture. This is exactly what the former renowned Televangelist; Billy Graham did during his crusades in the eighties and nineties.

This is the same way many Pentecostal and spiritual Churches pass to baptize people in the spirit. The Lord Jesus disapprove of this apostasy because He did not teach us to do that. Let's have a final look at what the Lord says about the Spirit baptism.

"The wind blows where it wants, (means the Holy Spirit searches the mind, heart and soul of all those who are ready for the new birth). "And you hear the sound thereof" (Means that the Holy Spirit is also a living God, who speaks and acts).

The scripture phrase doesn't mean that the Holy Spirit makes sounds or noise when coming to baptize someone. This is not true. "You hear the sound thereof" also means that the Holy Spirit speaks to us after He has baptized us.

"But cannot tell where it comes from, and where it goes" also means that no one knows the residence of the Holy Spirit, and none of us have seen Him before. Therefore, any pastor who says in a prayer, "Holy Ghost come now and baptize my members" is a liar from Satan.

The Spirt does not take command from any man dead or living, except from the Lord God and the Lord Jesus. This implies that it's a wrong approach to pray asking God or the Lord Jesus to let the Holy Spirit come and baptize someone. Only apostate pastors and ministers of God would do that.

I beg you; don't throw any stone yet until you have completed reading this book to know the reason why I say this. Scripture can never conflict itself except you, who with frail minds lean upon your only misunderstanding.

"So is every one that is born of the Spirit." This last phrase concludes whatever I have said above and means that if you claim you are born again, then it shouldn't come from any wrong means, but through the recommended ways given by the Lord Jesus. If therefore you claim to be born-again, then it should be through these ways:

- ❖ No one born of the Spirit commanded the Spirit or prayed to God for the Spirt to come and baptize him or her. The spirt came on His own discretion after seeing that you have followed the recommended criteria for receiving the born-again certificate.
- ❖ The person after receiving the Spirt birth hears the voice of the Holy Spirt.
- ❖ "So is everyone that is born of the Spirt" meaning that if your born-again came through a different process other than the above two, then your claim of being born again is sham.

From the above Bible quote, one can see that Nicodemus has some little doubts because the Lord had said, "The wind blows where it wants, and you hear the sound thereof, but cannot tell where it comes from."

Without the guidance of the holy Spirt, I would agree with Nicodemus because how can the wind (The Holy Spirt) blows (baptize) where it wants (the one He chooses to baptize even if the person is known to be sinner.)

The Lord Jesus loved him because of his believe in Him and wanted to initiate him into Christianity and to give him the Spirit birth. The Lord Jesus loves you the same way and for that matter, He's coming to teach you also to understand this Christian concept.

Let's listen to Nicodemus again as he asks the second most wisest question ever asked in the history of man.

> John Chapter 3:9. "Nicodemus answered and said unto him, how can these things be?"

This question posed by Nicodemus means that he has moved a step in understanding. He now accepts that the new-birth is a new concept, which the Lord has given to humanity. He understands that the Lord Jesus is introducing this new concept for his followers who want to "see" the Kingdom of God, and to "enter" into it.

What Nicodemus must do as a learned lawyer, a member of the ruling council of Israel, and a prior master of divine things about God is to ask this question and remain calm and listen to how the Lord Jesus would explain.

Should he find some fault somewhere, he will simply attack, abandon the Lord Jesus and go his way. Should the explanation to his question find a good place in his heart, he has learned a new concept that can enable him to "see" and to "enter" into the Kingdom of God.

For he had in the past days heard the Lord Jesus condemning the Pharisees that they were blind teachers who knew nothing about the Kingdom of God. Nicodemus memorized in retrospect one of the statements of condemnation by the Lord Jesus:

> "For I say unto you, That except your righteousness shall exceed the righteousness of the scribes and Pharisees, ye shall in no case enter into the kingdom of heaven."
>
> Matthew 5: 11.

Some of these sayings by the Lord Jesus were heart-troubling and a threat to the beliefs of the Pharisees regarding eternal life. Nicodemus being a Pharisee knows that there are sets of formalities and conditions for entry into the Kingdom of God, and these were the exact beliefs the Pharisees were practicing.

Apart from these laid down formalities, from where could the wind blow to, where shall it go, and upon whom shall it fall apart from them and their cronies who were known to be righteous and considered to be on the rightful path into the Kingdom of God?

In other words, where can another set of rules for entry into the Kingdom of God come from and who else apart from them can receive this new birth. Above all, how can anybody at all who does not practice a righteous life get this new birth to enter into the Kingdom of God?

Self-acclaimed righteous man as Nicodemus and his colleagues would among other things in those days, pray two hours non-stop every day in the temple of God. They fasted twice a week, and offered alms to the poor.

What more? They paid tithe on everything they received as income including even 'mint,' and 'anise,' and *cummin*, and offered regular sacrifices according to the customs of the Mosaic Law. Which other thing do they lack which can prevent them from seeing or entering into the Kingdom of God?

I tell you, all of us are guilty of the born-again concept. Most of us have approached the born-again concept with self-righteousness, riches, nobility and popularity in the Church like Nicodemus. However, none of these can lead to born-again.

The Lord knows Nicodemus as one of those who taught the people of Israel deeper things about God in the temple. If he does not know how one can enter into the Kingdom of God, apart from the old ways he knows, then he must humble himself like a child because much learning and pride does not take people into this kingdom.

He wants to tell Nicodemus as well as countless Christians living today and those to come in the future that entry into the Kingdom of God hinges on obedience to the Word of God. In the book of Matthew, the Lord tells us the type of obedience we need before we can receive the new-birth:

> "Verily I say unto you, Except ye be converted, and become as little children, ye shall not enter into the kingdom of heaven."
>
> Matthew 18: 3.

To become "as a little child" before getting the Kingdom of God means to forget all the rot teachings you have compiled about this concept and behave as if you had never heard about it before. This is the only condition to receive the truth.

The Lord Jesus is now attacking Nicodemus who is dumbfounded with sporadic bombardment of scriptural truth that has never be penned down in any religious book before. When God speaks, the whole world remains silent before Him.

The Lord Jesus, the master of the Day of Judgment is speaking. The one with control over death is telling Nicodemus as well as entire humanity plainly that book knowledge and worldly wisdom has nothing to do with the wisdom of God. This is how he openly and thoughtfully flamed the sentence:

> John Chapter 3:10 "Are you a master of Israel and you do not know these things?"

"The master of Israel" is a learned person placed in high position to teach the Israelites the Mosaic Law and the way of God during the Old Testament times. The master of Israel is also a member of the Sanhedrin, the ruling class of Israel.

The Lord is asking Nicodemus, a full lawyer, a cabinet minister and a religious guru whether he has not the wisdom to discern the meaning when God speaks. The same way, this statement by the Lord is telling notorious academicians, top politicians, business tycoons and cultist masters, that their false religions, academic credentials and authority have failed them.

The simple reason is that you claim to know all the mysteries about creation, but being so foolish, all your knowledge shall end up in the grave. Some of you have sold their soul for power, prosperity and fame and have more than you desired.

By the help of demons and evil ways, some of you have all that you want in this short life, forgetting your creator, and the simple command He gives you to become born-again. Your motto is "Do art thou wilt," even at the expense of others lives.

This motto shall turn into strong chains and the same shall be used to hang your neck whilst you wait impatiently in that dangerous dungeon in eternity until judgment day. You glutton, and a capital fool! If you have no heart to discern the truth, haven't you eyes to see the end of the scornful ones?

Christians however says that "if in this life only we have hope in Christ, we are of all men most miserable." (1 Corinthians 15:19). This makes Christianity the most enviable worship on this planet. This is also the reason why these cultists who have sold their souls to the devil are always seeking to destroy Christianity.

8

ONLY THE LORD JESUS GIVES THE SPIRIT BIRTH

The more the Lord Jesus conversed with Nicodemus, the more He became charged in the spirit exposing His countenance as the Word of John 1:1. At this point, we see the Lord Jesus moving deeper into mysteries and addressing Nicodemus:

> John Chapter 3:11 "Verily, verily, I say unto thee, we speak what we know, and testify what we have seen; and you receive not our witness."

We see the Lord Jesus at this point speaking on behalf of the three Godhead, the Holy Trinity of which He is a prior member. According to the above scripture, the Lord Jesus is speaking about what He knows and testifying to the source from where this born-again concept came from.

According to Him, He was there as one of the key members of the three everlasting powers of creation when the concept born-again was decreed as the only entry condition into the Kingdom of God for humanity.

Therefore, if it's the Kingdom of God that you desire, then you must be born-again. If you don't desire the Kingdom of God, you can continue with your ass. In addition, if at this point of your life you want to make a quick turnaround from the wrong religion you are in, it's not too late.

The Lord Jesus shall welcome you. It doesn't matter the level of your filth and blasphemy. The Lord wants people like you. If you're a Christian worshipping with any Church that doesn't teach this born-again, I urge you to quit no matter how committed you have been to them and the position you hold there.

It's all about your single soul. You need to preserve it well by struggling for the truth like this one so that you do not lose it to Satan. Be on the alert. Never lose guard in these last days, and don't be a respecter of pastors, Church elders and those who weird power over you, whose spiritual background you do not know.

They count nothing before the Lord Jesus and value nothing before sincere Christian believers. The Lord Jesus is coming and that everybody is preparing to meet Him, so don't waste time in Churches where the Gospel of Christ is not preached and the mystery of the Kingdom of God taught.

You must get control over your own life and soul now that you're alive and strong. In eternity, you may not have this opportunity. If you don't act swiftly and wisely now, you may die without being born-again. This shall be an abominable thing for your soul.

Many people will regret in eternity for not receiving the new-birth when the Lord Jesus on the last day shall say to them; "I tell you, I know you not whence ye are; depart from me, all ye workers of iniquity." (Luke 13:27). When this happens to you, where shall you go? There would be no place to turn than to enter hellfire.

Water baptism is the old one we all know. Many people after getting this do not proceed further to getting the spirit-birth, which is the most important. If you're someone serious to enter into the Kingdom of God, you must enforce the one who gives you the water birth to show you the rightful way to receive the spirit-birth as well.

Much has been said about the spirit-birth, but we don't know who is responsible for giving this birth. John the Baptist, the forerunner of the Lord Jesus told us about these types of two births and pointed to the one who gives the Spirit birth.

He made it clear that he baptizes with water, but the Lord Jesus shall baptize with the spirit.

> "I indeed baptize you with water unto repentance: but he that comes after me is mightier than I, whose shoes I am not worthy to untie: he shall baptize you with the Holy Spirit, and with fire."
>
> Matthew 3:11.

John baptized with water for repentance of sin, but he told us that the Lord Jesus shall baptize his followers with the Holy Spirit and with fire. This scripture affirms that the Spirit baptism is the most important, and it's only the Lord Jesus who gives this kind of birth.

Coming back to our main point, the Lord Jesus has told Nicodemus that He was there at the meeting when the new-birth was instituted in

Heaven as the only entry permit into the Kingdom of God. Whether Nicodemus agrees or not, what is decreed is decreed.

The whole lesson was like a university professor teaching a class one boy addition and multiplication. He teaches the boy that $2+2 = 4$; and $2 \times 2 = 4$. If there should be any better explanation, it should center on how the answer was derived, but not why the two answers should be the same.

Nicodemus still had some doubts in his mind, but I can't tell whether he needed some further clarification on born-again or he doubted the Lord Jesus for saying that He was in Heaven when the concept was instituted for humanity.

If you study humans very carefully, you notice that most of you do not like the truth, but lies. You visit fetish shrines where spirits reveal themselves and talk to you. You visit places where dwarfs perform magic in the presence of a large cloud bringing to life things the magician commands to appear on stage.

You visit spiritualist who make spirits talk. At such places, you are keen to hear these infernal spirits predict a good future and a better life for you. You believe all these bunch of abominations wholeheartedly, but for the Lord Jesus to say that He came from Heaven has become a riddle to Nicodemus and the unbelieving world including you.

Had Nicodemus forgotten about the many prophecies about the Lord Jesus, which he's very conversant with? Nicodemus must not doubt God. You believe God today, and disbelieve Him tomorrow. Is Nicodemus not the same person who declared; "We know that thou art a teacher come from God?"

This admission by Nicodemus meant that he, as well as his learned, friends knew that Jesus came from God. If they believe this, where lays the basis for his doubt. Had the Lord Jesus said He came from Satan, you will see how the whole world would have rushed on Him. No wonder, the Lord said:

> "I am come in my Father's name, and ye receive me not: if another shall come in his own name, him ye will receive."
>
> John 5:43.

The Lord made this prediction about the Antichrist; leader of the soon coming New World Order. Some seventy years after his ascension, the Lord again revealed information about this man of sin in the book of Revelation

> "And all that dwell upon the earth shall worship him, whose names are not written in the book of life of the Lamb slain from the foundation of the world."
>
> Revelation 13:8.

Coming back to Nicodemus, the Lord Jesus pitied him for his doubts (not unbelieve) and decided to help him so that he can know the in-and-out of born-again. At this point, the Lord Jesus seeking to know the final stance of Nicodemus authoritatively declared:

> Chapter 3:12 "If I have told you earthly things, and you do not believe, how shall you believe, if I tell you of heavenly things?"

According to the Lord Jesus, as far as information about God and His kingdom is concerned, born-again is the least information everybody is supposed to believe easily. Therefore, anyone who refuses this simple message doesn't deserve to know the mystery about the Kingdom of God.

If you don't believe this simple information, how can you believe when He tells you for instance that there are mighty and sophisticated angelic aircraft in the Kingdom of Heaven which the Lord's angels use each time they come on mission to planet earth.

What, if He tells you that the sea of glass in the front of the Throne of God is a giant heavenly monitor screen, which captures the image of every creature living in God's created earth. How can we believe the fact that planet earth is not spinning like a ball as has been alleged and documented in all text books, but it's flat?

I want to share with you a simple mystery to clarify what the Lord Jesus said to Nicodemus. In the book of Revelation, the Word of God tells us; "Blessed is he that readeth, and they that hear the words of this prophecy, and keep those things which are written therein." (Revelation 1:3).

Look at a strange book, which blesses both readers and those who listen to people who read it. Despite such an open invitation to blessings, Christians do not read this book. This is a big shame on all Christians; and a double shame to all those who claim to be born-again, but are not.

It's an indictment on pastors who think they are born-again, but are not. Through their deceptive teachings or ignorance, millions of

Christians have over looked or ignored an open invitation to God's blessings.

So many Christians in these last days turn to these pastors and sham men of God with their problems which solutions never come. You prefer what pastors tell you to reading the Bible. Meanwhile, it's only the Bible that shows humans the true picture of God and his creation.

Driving my point home, I want you to bear with me that Nicodemus was a godly man who was very conversant with all the entry conditions into the Kingdom of God through the mosaic laws and the traditions of the Jews.

He was not conversant with the precepts of this new decree, and for that matter, it is obvious that he wasn't born-again before and during the time of his conversation with the Lord. For that matter, he lacked the receptacle (God's spirit) to enable him understand mysteries.

It is the same with millions of Christians who attend Churches today. Most of you are not born-again and because of that you look, but can't see. You listen, but can't hear, neither do you understand.

Notwithstanding, the Lord Jesus wants to move higher into mysteries which neither Nicodemus nor you is supposed to hear, but for the love He has for Nicodemus, the world and you, He will disclose how one can become born-again.

If you enjoy this book and have accepted its contents up to this point, then I am happy for you because we're now entering into mysteries about born-again. If there is any point you did not grasp well, you must go back and read again because this can hinder your understanding of the rest of the book.

9

THE LORD JESUS TEACHES HOW ONE CAN BECOME BORN-AGAIN

At this point during the discussion with Nicodemus, the Lord Jesus saw that Nicodemus had grasped the fact that born-again is a new religious concept, which He's introducing into the world. He now proves to Nicodemus the source from where this concept came:

> John Chapter 3:13 "And no man hath ascended up to heaven, but he that came down from heaven, even the Son of man which is in heaven."

Jesus is saying that no man born of a woman has power whatsoever to ascend into Heaven to tap information for men. The Lord Jesus proved to Nicodemus straight away that He resided in Heaven and descended from there to teach the world the way into the Kingdom of God.

We were all born into this world as part of God's creation, but in the case of the Lord Jesus, He is one of the members of the Holy Trinity. The Lord Jesus indeed is God. He is the 'I am' of Exodus 3:14; John 8:58; and the "Word" of John 1:1. If you believe this, then you are on the rightful path to receiving the new-birth.

Some cold wind might have blown upon Nicodemus making him to listen to the Lord Attentively. He might be recollecting all the information about the Lord Jesus recorded in the Bible in retrospect. He has never seen someone come down from Heaven before. I am sure he looked at the Lord Jesus sternly, again, and again.

Throughout their conversation, Nicodemus never questioned the Lord about his deity. He dare not do so because anyone who heard Jesus' message testified that He was God on earth. Angels were always on guard and the Spirit of God always round about Him until the day He ascended back into Heaven.

We can't forget the strange eclipse that occurred on the day of crucifixion neither the earthquake that occurred around the temple and tore the temple veil into two when the Lord was demonstrating to humanity there was life after death.

Remember the transfiguration and the wonderful appearance of Moses and Elias in a mini-spaceship, which the Bible calls "Cloud of heaven." Remember how Peter and John became amazed and frightened when they saw it compelling them to ask the Lord whether they should build three tabernacles at the spot.

Nothing of the sort happened during the Lord's conversation with Nicodemus, but I tell you, the grounds could be shaken, and the room tense with milliards of by-passing angels. I am saying this because, this was the time the actual key, which opens the doors to the Kingdom of God, was going to be given to humanity.

Without this particular key (detailed information on born-again), the Lord Jesus' visit to earth could have been meaningless. The Lord Jesus on that day was reconciling humanity to God. He was breaking the barrier between humanity and God, which forbid us to become the sons of God. This implied that He was telling humanity to admit their sinful nature and say "Enough" to sins so that they can acknowledge God as their creator.

He would neither invite the Chief priest, the high priest, the Pharisees, the Sadducees, the writers of the law popularly called scribes nor any other dignitaries of His time because none of them worth the occasion.

God used Nicodemus alone in this grandeur ceremony to demonstrate that Born-again is between God and humanity. In this short, but grandeur ceremony, the Lord Jesus represented God and the heavenly Hosts, and Nicodemus represented humanity to sign this agreement.

The details of the agreement was that from that particular hour, the nation Israel was not the only nation God acknowledges as His nation. From that hour, the decree was that any human born to this earth both those alive and those to be born later, whether black or white, from the North or South, from the East or West, we must all admit to the following:

- ❖ That the Lord God is a creator of all things
- ❖ That from that very hour onwards, anyone who wants to honor God must honor the Lord Jesus. (John 5:23).
- ❖ That He God is reconciling the nations of the whole world unto Himself through the Lord Jesus.
- ❖ That He has plans for every human living or yet to be born.
- ❖ That this plan is to settle humans in an everlasting place in eternity called the Kingdom of God.
- ❖ That anyone who wants to enter into the Kingdom of God must be born-again.

- ❖ That humanity must obey the conditions attached to born-again, which is to "believe" in the name of the Lord Jesus who is disclosing this information written in this agreement.
- ❖ That to prove the existence of the Kingdom of God in eternity, where the dead ones in him shall go, He will let the Lord Jesus demonstrate to the whole world that there is resurrection of the dead.

This extravaganza ceremony was the hour of redemption for humanity. The very hour from where the Lord Jesus would be granting the new-birth to individual Christians who want to enter into the Kingdom of God.

Nicodemus couldn't see anything going on around him because he was at that time engulfed in pride, and misconception of scriptural truth. He never saw one angel nor any changes in the face of the Lord Jesus, but I tell you, something very serious was going on.

You are equally naïve to this great occasion, but unlike Nicodemus who was defending God at the time, you are defending a Church established by someone whose identity or history you do not know. You are not only proud, but someone contending against the truth.

Whether you believe this or not, God launched this grandeur ceremony to inform humanity that His doors were opened to everyone on earth who wants to become His son. Your pride and contentious mind can't change God's plans.

Having known why and how the born-again concept reached the hands of humanity, I am sure you will try to defend and spread it. For the power it weirds, no one can belittle this subject on born-again and go scot-free.

If you have aided some Church in any way to explain away this all-important concept you are doomed forever, and it would be better if you were not born into this world. However, if you repent of this sin, the Lord will forgive you.

Judas Iscariot took bribe because of jealousy for money and betrayed the Lord Jesus in fulfillment of prophecy. It never ended up well with him. He is in torment wherever he may be whilst the stiffer punishment awaits him in hellfire.

If you have also taken bribe from any quarters to adulterate the gospel, your case could be worse than Judas' own. You fool, the Bible talks about you:

> "For what is a man profited, if he shall gain the whole world, and lose his own soul? Or what shall a man give in exchange for his soul?"
>
> Matthew 16:26, 27.

You always hear and see how swindle televangelists scream on television stations that the Lord Jesus never asked anyone to become born-again. They say this openly before their followers who nod heads and clap hands in applause.

Today, you have that big mouth to say whatever you want, but in a short time, illness, old age or death shall silence or bungle you into the grave to be interrogated by the Lord's angels. At this time, you will shut that big mouth and stop disturbing humanity.

After death, your much learning, big titles, foolish pride, massive wealth, and smart security guards can never save you. Underground bunkers can never hide you. The CERN cannon can never protect you neither the Cult Church you established or served.

Over there in the grave, all the vain words you used against the Lord Jesus and His kingdom shall be visible to you. The money some of you took to corrupt the Bible and what you extorted from Church members and the general public in the name of Jesus shall turn into spiritual abominations upon your head.

This shall continue to hunt and torment you until judgment day when all sinners shall appear before the judgment seat of the Lord Jesus Christ for the final judgment. This is the time you will see and feel the impact of the harm you did to your fellow humans.

You feel strong, proud and bold to corrupt the Bible. You count yourself as one of the millionaires who enjoy a healthy life. You look handsome and beautiful, smart, powerful, and someone enjoying your exuberant youth like Joyce Meyers and Joel Oesten today.

You have amassed mansions, jets, cars and properties like T.D. Jakes or Benny Hinn. You can continue to make your false claims of ascending and descending the ladder of Heaven where you claim to meet and Chat with the Almighty God and the Lord Jesus like the Angel Obinim of Ghana.

You can scramble for the topmost Christian titles and supersede all the titles by choosing the title "angel" upon yourself like Reverend *Obofo* of Ghana and Angel Obinim. You can teach the prosperity gospel and flow with better English grammar more than Mensah Otabil of Ghana flows.

You can pray with tongues and command God to respond to your prayer more constantly than Duncan William also of Ghana. You can claim to heal, and do more powerful miraculous works than T.B. Joshua of Nigeria.

You can also distribute millions of free monthly devotional booklets like Pastor Christ or share free Bibles and literature more than the Jehovah Witness, but don't forget one thing before you depart from planet earth.

Many people wonder why the Lord would not take action now against such spiritual wickedness perpetrated against the people of the world. Others boil up to the point that if they had the chance, they could strike against these blasphemers and apostate Christians.

Angel Obinim of Ghana stood in his Church temple and insulted the Almighty God and the Lord Jesus for not killing him if he were not working for them. Meanwhile, his beliefs, and practices as a founder of a Church isn't in line with the norms of a true Christian Church.

Because nothing happened to him, his blind and dumb followers, who have been hypnotized and mesmerized think all is well. There is time for everything, and for each of these sham men of God.

When death knocks at your door, and you see him face-to-face coming to take you away, you will respect God and the Lord Jesus. Today, you are like King Belshazzar who never respected God.

You big fool! You can continue to enjoy your ill-acquired wealth, and admire your wife and girlfriends. You can continue to talk big, but very soon, the writing shall be on your wall:

MENE, MENE, TEKEL, UPHARSIN.

Daniel 5: 25.

I know you are one of these sham men of God who want to attack this truthful message about born-again. I know you are part of the team that has shrouded born-again in secrecy and hidden its meaning, significance and importance from those around you and the rest of the world.

Don't forget that no matter what you do to corrupt this born-again concept, the Lord knows His own and how to save them. He will continue to do this until all His elected ones are sealed with the power of born-again.

Now consider this! Nicodemus is not a small boy who could not speak his mind if what the Lord Jesus told him were not the absolute truth he wanted. Once Nicodemus couldn't challenge, who are you to intervene.

When the Almighty God, the Lord Jesus and the Holy Spirit institute a concept that Christians must observe in order to enter into the Kingdom of God. Who are you to say no? Your resistance can't stop God's plans.

The Lord Jesus says born-again is the only entry permit into the Kingdom of God. Nicodemus has succumbed to this fact. I have also done my best to explain it to you. It will be unwise on your part to follow any dead Church which teaches a different born-again.

The Satanist elite and these sham men of God call you *goyim*, useless eater, sheep and man of sorrow. They are the very people who formed most of the Churches you attend. Instead, for you to sit back and reason for yourself, you defend these rocks when their mission is only to blaspheme the name of God and pervert the gospel.

The Word of God combines you with these sham men of God and urges you to think and think deeply about this important scripture once again:

> "For what is a man profited, if he shall gain the whole world, and lose his own soul? Or what shall a man give in exchange for his soul?"
>
> Matthew 16: 26.

My beloved ones, your single soul is very precious to the Lord Jesus. He wants you to come and enjoy a better rest in paradise. He wants you to think carefully about your single soul and how you are playing with it because of money, which doesn't last forever.

Come home and reason like Nicodemus who now understands the concept of born-again. He is speechless and anxious to hear more about how one can become born-again. He wished he had been baptized to become born-again.

At this point whether you are a pastor or someone who claim to know more about born-again, I am sure you are also quiet and ready to know the processes through which one can become born-again. However, before I Continue, let's pray.

> The Lord Jesus; the Word of God. You who was in the beginning with God.

You who made all things; and without you was not anything made that was made.
You who descended down to earth because of your love for humanity.

You who came to earth purposely to reconcile the world to the Lord God.
You who came to demonstrate the Kingdom of God to humanity.
You who came to show humanity the entry condition into the Kingdom of God.

I humbly pray to you to give the reader of this book and anyone who will hear this truthful message a new heart and spirit, and grant them to know the process to become born-again so that they can be born-again. I ask this in the name of the father, and of the Son and of the Holy Ghost, Amen.

At this particular moment, the Lord Jesus has sent the Comforter to guide and lead you to understand the concept of born-again. The Lord Jesus is now coming to show you how a Christian can receive the Spirit-birth.

I am continuing with the conversation between the Lord Jesus and Nicodemus. The Lord Jesus is coming to refer Nicodemus to an incidence in the wilderness at the time when the nation Israel were moving from the land of Egypt to the Promised Land.

> John Chapter 3:14 "And as Moses lifted up the serpent in the wilderness, even so must the Son of man be lifted up."

The Lord Jesus has quoted from the book of Numbers 21: 9 to illustrate how we can receive the Spirit birth. Nicodemus might marvel for hearing this scripture, which he's so familiar with. Let's quickly go through this short Bible account and find out why the Lord quoted from the book of Numbers.

During the exodus, when Moses was leading the Israelites from Egypt to the Promised Land, the people spoke against God, and Moses, saying:

> "Why have you brought us out of Egypt to die in the wilderness? For there is no bread, neither is there any water and we can die here."

> Numbers 21: 5.

This was an accusation against the Lord God. It was a speech of defiant and apostasy. How could God bring His own people unto the wilderness to kill them? Is He not the same God who delivered them from bondage in Egypt?

The people of Israel murmured this because they had forgotten about the ten powerful plaques, which fostered their immediate release from bondage on the land of Egypt? They had also forgotten the manner that fell daily from Heaven to feed them on the wilderness.

Being so ungrateful, they had forgotten how they at a point in time became thirsty on the wilderness, and how God through Moses, miraculously made water flow from a dumb rock, which they drank to quench their thirst.

If God could do all these things to their attestation, from where came such ungrateful statement. Our modern day televangelists and some Christians act the same way like those disgruntled Israelites.

So many Christians today murmur at the least problem and say God had been ungrateful to them.

The Israelites were ungrateful, and for being so, the Lord God decided to punish them. The lord let fiery serpents bit them; and many people of Israel died.

The death rate increased day-by-day until they could not control the situation. When the people saw that they have spoken against the LORD, and against Moses; they asked Moses to pray to the Lord to take away the serpents from them. Moses accepted their plea and prayed for them.

The LORD God accepted their repentance and commanded Moses to make a "fiery serpent," and set it upon a pole so that anyone bitten by the snakes when he looks upon it shall live. Moses did as the Lord commanded him, and it happened that if a serpent had bitten any man, when he raised his head to watch the brass serpent, he lived.

Why did the Lord Jesus mention or chipped in this information during his conversation with Nicodemus? There is a real issue surrounding this snakebite and the brass snake, which was hanged on the tree. That brass snake built by Moses on the wilderness was the Lord Jesus himself.

According to scriptures, if a serpent had bitten any man, when he raised his head to watch the brass serpent, he lived. They were healed because of BELIEVE. No medicine, no holy water, no anointing oil, no incense, no candle, no all-night, no special prayers, but through simple BELIEVE.

This same Jesus has now come in a human form and is telling people who want eternal life to "believe" in Him so that they can become born-again, to enable them "to see" and "to enter" into the Kingdom of God.

Now, look at the true picture. The Israelites looked at the raised brass serpent and by believing, they got healed from bites from poisonous serpents. This could not grant them to "see" or "enter" into the Kingdom of God.

The Lord Jesus says, "Believe" in me and you shall have eternal life. Is eternal life not worth more than recovery from snakebite? If this is so, why are the people of this world feeling reluctant to "believe" the one who cares for the world and sacrificed Himself for us?

Why are modern pastors calling people to have a holi spirit, holi water, and all sorts of toys and forms claiming these could save them? Why have Churches banished every information about born-again?

All what the Lord Jesus wants to say is that if the Israelites who "believed" looked at the raised serpent and were saved after snake had bitten them; then any person on earth who "believes" in his (Jesus') name shall also be saved to "enter" and to "see" the Kingdom of God.

Nicodemus as well as all Israelis knew and believed this true Bible account. The Lord chipped in this short history during their conversation to remind him about the importance of another Christian concept, "Believe."

These poisonous snakes were spread everywhere on the wilderness, and anyone they bit never survived life. So many Israelites who were vexed with Moses would not look at the brass serpent in order to be saved.

It is the same with the world today. False religions as well as false Christian Churches spread across the globe doesn't teach born-again. These Churches are poisonous than those serpents on the wilderness.

The least careless mistake one makes, they bite you, and because their members do not believe in the Lord Jesus, they die without eternal life. It is no exaggeration to say that millions and millions of people who professed to be Christians had been bitten by these false teachings and have died and gone to the grave without becoming born-again.

Over there, there is no repentance or turning back again. They have no second chance to become born-again. They will come out one day from their dungeons in the underworld, only to be judged according to the law on born- again and be dumped in hellfire.

Thanks to the Lord God. It's not all the people of Israel who died from the snakebites. The brass snake raised on the cross came to save those who "believed." If Moses had hidden the brass snake at a corner for the people to walk long distances, or queue before catching a glimpse of it, most of them might have lost their lives.

The best way was to hang it on a raised tree so that wherever a snake victim was located; as soon as the person raised his or her head, he could catch a glimpse of the brass snake and become saved.

In the same way, the Lord Jesus is raised for all.

His message has gone to all the uttermost parts of the world for people to know and believe in him so that they can receive the new-birth. This requires no righteousness or good works. Like the brass snake on the wilderness, any Christian who "believes" the Lord Jesus receives the new-birth.

The key phrase in this true Bible account is "a raised brass snake" that could save snake bitten victims. The key word is also "Believe" that once a snake victim looks at the raised brass snake, the person is saved.

Now, after the Lord has chipped in this true Bible account in the conversation, He continued to show Nicodemus, you, and the entire world how to receive the Spirit-birth. Let's look at the full sentence again;

> Chapter 3:14 "And as Moses lifted up the serpent in the wilderness, even so must the Son of man be lifted up."

The Lord Jesus predicted His death when He said he was going to be lifted up like how Moses raised the brass snake on the wilderness. The Lord used to talk about His crucifixion on the cross, which according to Him was going to be greater in importance than the brass snake raised on the tree.

Let's affirm this with another prediction the Lord made later in the book of John concerning His crucifixion in the same book:

> "And I, if I be lifted up from the earth, will draw all men unto me."

John 12:32.

The Lord says He will "draw all men" unto himself. All men here means the entire human race, not the people of Israel only. This is the reason why His crucifixion was more important than the raised snake that could only save snake bitten victims on the wilderness.

According to the Lord Jesus, as soon as he is raised on the cross, those who shall "believe" in Him shall be saved. The crucifixion means that the Lord Jesus accomplished his mission on earth. He finished his part of the contract to teach humanity the way into the Kingdom of God.

The other side of the salvation contract is left with those desirous to "see" and to "enter" into the Kingdom of God to fulfill theirs. If you are confused, let me come down more to enable you understand this.

The Lord Jesus is telling you that when humanity sees that He is crucified on the cross, His powers and ministry doesn't end there, but rather it is the time that those who are seeking for entry into the Kingdom of God must do something.

Let's have a look at what we must do after the Lord is crucified on the cross. This takes us to the continuation of the Lord's conversation with Nicodemus:

> John Chapter 3:15 "That whosoever believes in him should not perish, but have eternal life."

The word once again is "Believe". Anyone who believes in the Lord Jesus Christ shall never be condemned into hell fire, but shall have eternal life. The Israelis "believed" in the brass snake hanged on a tree on the wilderness and were saved.

This time around, we are not commanded to "believe" in a brass snake. We are not commanded to bow down before Fatima or Mary. We are not commanded to roll on the ground or to serve a pastor in order to be saved.

We are not commanded to use holi oil in order to become saved. We are also not commanded to pray, fast, pay more tithe, or acquire any holi spirit before we can be saved. The lord Jesus did not tell us to use the sticker of any prophet apostle or an angel. He says we should "believe" in him.

The Lord Jesus says "whosoever" shall "believe" in him shall be saved. "Whosoever" here means that getting eternal life is not selective, but indiscriminate. It is open to every human no matter what the level of your sins. The Lord Jesus has shown you how to receive the new-birth. It is simple arithmetic.

If you truly "believe" the Lord Jesus, you get this new-birth. If you don't "believe" him, you shall be cast outside of the Kingdom of God. Allow the Lord Jesus to explain further as He continues His conversation with Nicodemus:

> Chapter 3:16 "For God so loved the world, that he gave his only begotten Son, that whosoever believes in him should not perish, but have everlasting life."

If you have noticed very carefully, you could see that from the last few pages, I have been hammering on the word "believe" several times. However, it's now that the concept itself has cropped up in its proper place in the conversation with Nicodemus. Let's take the scripture again:

> "For God so loved the world that he gave his only begotten Son, that whosoever believes in him should not perish, but have everlasting life."

In the above golden verse, what the Lord Jesus wants everybody to know is that Satan had wanted to destroy the entire human race and push all of us into hellfire. God, being our creator who loves us sent the Lord Jesus to the earth to announce the Kingdom of God and to show us the entry conditions.

The entry condition is a command, which says, "Ye must be born again," which in other words means that it is compulsory for everybody on earth to be born-again if the person wants to enter into the Kingdom of God. The next condition is that if you want to become born-again, you must "believe" the Lord Jesus.

As soon as you believe the Lord Jesus sincerely from your heart, He grants you the new-birth. To "believe" in the Lord Jesus has raised another scriptural complication, which by the power of the Comforter, I will explain in the latter part of this book.

The Bible quote above has shown Nicodemus as well as you and me what we must do to receive the new-birth. The whole secret lies in the concept "believe." If we now understand why we should "believe" in the Lord Jesus, let's hear the ensuing conversation between the Lord Jesus and Nicodemus:

> John Chapter 3:17 "For God sent not his Son into the world to condemn the world; but that the world through him might be saved."

When the Lord came down to earth, He neither discriminated against nor condemned anyone. In our modern world, when someone commits a small or serious crime, there is always a public outcry for severe punishment for this person.

This is not all. Governments, worldwide, have set up prison centers where they punish sinners. People who commit trivial offences needing pardon are not spared. If you go to some prisons, you could see condemned prisoners who have spent all their lives in deprived conditions without anybody having pity on them.

Here comes the owner of the world by whom all things were created ((John 1:1–3)) who never drove away one sinner or criminal who came to him. He never set up prisons to punish any of these people or litigated with anybody that led to the person's imprisonment.

When the Lord Jesus came, He opened up his teachings to all people including sinners and the poor. He never discriminated against anyone. He came to save the witch, fetish priests, those possessed with demons, the spiritualist, fornicators, prostitutes, liars, thieves, drunkards, murderers and adulterers.

He also came to save the idolater and all kinds of sinners. The Lord Jesus doesn't condemn anybody. He admits all manner of people into his kingdom, no matter how big or serious your sins are. All you need to do is to "believe" in Him and become born-again.

The Lord Jesus was indeed, a great man when He came to this earth. No man had ever lived on earth; and there is none to come after him who would be famous, popular, and greater than Him in stature, in power, in glory and in fame.

His fame and nobility followed Him wherever He went. Everybody who heard his name sought for Him. They hailed him like a King. For one or two occasions, He withdrew to a far land to avoid being taken as a King of the Jews.

Besides His greatness, He was God incarnate. This man mingled with all manner of persons as he walked the streets of towns and villages in ancient Israel. He was nicknamed the lover of sinners. For sure, it is indisputable that the Lord Jesus loves you more than you love yourself.

We read earlier that at any time in the Bible when a statement of "Believe" in the Lord Jesus is expressed before Him; He decreed eternal life upon the person. When Zacchaeus met the Lord Jesus, he repented of his sins and promised to give back half of his possessions to the poor.

This statement constituted strong believe in the Lord Jesus. Zacchaeus couldn't have made such an amazing pronouncement if he had not known who the Lord Jesus was. To clear all arguments about Zacchaeus' "believe," we all bear testimony to how he even addressed Jesus as Lord.

If Jesus was his Lord, then, he indeed, believed him:

> "And Zacchaeus stood, and said unto the Lord; Behold, Lord, the half of my goods I give to the poor; and if I have taken any thing from any man by false accusation, I restore him fourfold."
>
> Luke 19: 8.

Forbes report released in March 2017 stated that there are currently 2,043 U.S. dollar billionaires worldwide from sixty-six (66) countries, with a combined net worth of $7.67 trillion. You get that picture.

If half of them could promise to give back half of their possession to the poor, there would be no poverty for any nation on earth. There would be no disease, water shortages, energy crisis and housing problems anywhere on our planet.

Although they know the Lord Jesus and know specifically who He is. They know His commitment to the poor, and His command for the rich to help the poor, but they will never do what Zacchaeus did.

Zacchaeus was deeply convinced that Jesus was the promised Messiah who came to take away the sins of men. He read the Old Testament scriptures and knew more about the Lord Jesus. For that matter, I can say that he "believed" in the Lord Jesus.

He saw that giving half of his possession was not even enough to give to the poor. His conviction was based upon the Lord's lessons on Charity. He might have heard this teaching from some of the disciples.

He therefore promised that if he had by any foul means taken anything from anybody, he multiplies it by four and give it back to the person. He made this promise to express true repentance due to strong "believe" in the Lord Jesus as the son of God.

On seeing this strong believe, the Lord Jesus automatically baptized Zacchaeus with the new-birth and granted him eternal life when he said, "Salvation has come to your house today." (Luke 19:9). Once

Zacchaeus has believed in the Lord Jesus, he and his household have been saved.

There is a mystery, which I want to disclose to all of you. The mystery here is that anyone who becomes truly born-again receives it for himself or herself and the entire household. You may want biblical proof to this mystery.

When the Prison Keeper asked the Apostle Peter and Silas what he must do in order to be saved, their response was "Believe on the Lord Jesus Christ, and thou shalt be saved, and thy house."

Noah "believed" and he, together with his eight children were saved from the great flood. Lot "believed" and he, together with his wife and two children were saved from the fire of brimstone that destroyed the twin city of Sodom and Gomorrah.

We have similar instances in the Bible where the proclamation of "You and your household shall be saved" has been pronounced on different people in the book of Acts of the Apostles for those who "believed" the gospel facts about the Lord Jesus.

This is the affirmation that "God sent not his Son into the world to condemn the world; but that the world through him might be saved." Zacchaeus, a tax collector, considered to be wicked and a sinner in Israel at the time, was not condemned by the Lord, rather He granted him eternal life.

Saul, who became Paul was the persecutor of the Lord's disciples. The Lord Jesus did not condemn him. He was rather raised to become a living vessel upon whose shoulders we have most of the New Testament books.

The Lord Jesus does not condemn you as well. Whether you are a notorious armed robber or a prostitute, whether witchcraft or wizard, whether fraudster or drug pusher, whether gay or lesbian, the Lord Jesus needs you. All you have to do is to "believe" in him so that you can become born-again.

Born-again is not a common concept to joke with. It is the gift of God that comes with power to the recipient. Everybody must strive hard to receive this priceless gift of God for the benefit of his or her entire household.

Coming back to the conversation between the Lord Jesus and Nicodemus, we saw that Nicodemus first expressed "believe" in the Lord Jesus. This prompted the Lord Jesus to release to him the decree on born-again instituted by the Godhead.

Throughout the conversation, we see that Nicodemus is sober as the Lord teaches him. He wasn't sober for nothing. He mellowed himself in order to get the new-birth. Nicodemus later became a staunch Christian.

We read that when the Lord Jesus was crucified, Nicodemus went to ask for his dead body for burial. If at this time, you want to receive the new-birth like Zacchaeus, and Nicodemus, you can express a similar "believe" in the Lord Jesus.

You must act the same way these two men acted by humbling yourself and "believing" in the name of the Lord Jesus and you shall be born-again. Nicodemus knew what it is to "believe" in the Lord Jesus, and because of that, he did not ask any further questions.

If you also know how to "believe" in the name of the Lord Jesus, you have crossed from death to life and from hell to the Kingdom of God. On the other hand, if you don't know what it is to "believe" in the Lord Jesus, you must humble yourself and wait patiently until I have explained to you in this book.

10

THOSE WHO DO NOT BELIEVE ARE CONDEMNED

The Lord Jesus has brought His lessons on born-again to an end, but hasn't left hold of Nicodemus. He knows for sure that those who love Satan more than Him would not take this lesson serious.

According to the Lord Jesus, if you won't listen to Him, but would stick to the old information about born-again which you already know, it is your own soul and fate in eternity.

He has done His part. A student prepares for the lecturer and those who would not take the lecturer serious fail their exams. The Lord Jesus has told us that He is a sower who has gone out to sow. As He spreads the seeds; some will fall at the wayside.

Some will fall on rocks, some will fall on thorns, and the rest will fall in good soil. Choose to be the good soil not the bad one. The Lord Jesus has done His part by showing you and the world the only condition for entry into the Kingdom of God.

He wants to conclude His lessons on born-again, but before He does, He is telling Nicodemus as well as you:

> John Chapter 3:18 "He that believe on him (Jesus) is not condemned: but he that believe not is condemned already, because he hath not believed in the name of the only begotten Son of God."

The message is clear. You must choose to become a sincere Christian by believing in the Lord Jesus the rest of your life so that you can become born-again; or continue to believe the sham pastors running these cult Christian Churches and meet your condemnation in eternity.

11

NOT EVERY CHRISTIAN IS BORN-AGAIN

I will soon come to "believe" which is the most important ingredient in the preparation of the born-again soup, but before I do, let's catch a glimpse of some few important points. Many people were very close to the Lord Jesus and had an encounter with him during His ministry on earth, but were not saved.

The Pharisees as well as other Jews were close to Him all the time. They spoke to Him, and asked him questions on several occasions, but because they did not express "believe" in him, He didn't pronounce eternal life upon them.

The Lord Jesus pardoned the woman caught in prostitution who was dragged before Him. After she was delivered from her captors, the Lord asked her to go away, but not to sin again. (John 8:3-11). The ancient people of Israel would never spare someone caught live in prostitution.

No High priest could save such a person because of the people's zeal in protecting the Mosaic Law at that time. They would stone you alive. However, this prostitute woman was saved because of the powers of God.

You could see from the account that in spite of the wonderful way she was delivered from being stoned to death, this woman did not express any sign of believe in the Lord Jesus during her discourse with Him. For that matter, the Lord didn't pronounce eternal life upon her.

The Bible tells us about two men who were crucified close to the Lord Jesus. One on his right side and the other on the left side. The one on His right expressed believe in Him and was saved. The other on the left abused Him and was not saved. You get that.

Judas Iscariot was very close to the Lord Jesus, and of course, one of the twelve apostles. He walked, ate, and slept with the Lord Jesus. He was one of those who listened to information about the mysteries about the Kingdom of God, but because he didn't "believe" the Lord Jesus, he wasn't granted to become born-again to qualify for entry into the Kingdom of God.

It is the same with millions of Christians who attend different Churches today. They call the name of the Lord Jesus, but most of them are not born-again. This doesn't mean that they should stop going to Church. The Lord will have mercy upon those He will have mercy upon.

The problem comes from the Churches that people attend, and the pastors and teachers who teach them. It is obvious that most of them have hidden the truth from their members to remain in the Church until they pass away without receiving the new-birth.

How can the blind lead the blind, all of them shall fall into the ditch. How can the unlearned teach the unlearned and, how can the devil teach the sons of God the true gospel. If you are a member of any cult Church, it's high time you quit from them before it is too late for you.

Some of you are lucky to attend Churches where born-again is taught, but don't forget that a pastor or an evangelist may force you to accept Jesus Christ as your savior. You may repeat his salvation rhetoric several times, and continue to do it every day and for the rest of your life, but you can never become born-again. The reason is that the Lord didn't show his disciples this way.

Another sham man of God may take you through his so-called deliverance. He may invite some familiar spirit to cause you to shiver, scream, craw, limp, jump or rattle in strange tongue like as if you were a mad person.

He may spread his demonic hands upon you and cause you to fall. As you go through this trauma, you may think that you are born-again, but these are all wrong approach to born-again. A renowned Church may tell you that a born-again person is the one who speaks in tongues.

Because of that, their apostles or pastors may force you to learn how to speak false tongues. As soon as you are able to imitate others and begin to speak in false tongues, they will say you have been born-again. All these are sycophancy.

I tell you frankly that there is no other way to become born-again than what the Lord Jesus has taught us. This is to "believe" in the name of the Lord Jesus. You can only do this if you can manage to leave behind all the false teachings you know about this Christian concept taught you by the cult Church you attend.

To assist you identify false Churches and sham men of God, you must watch out for the following:

- ❖ fake miracle workers,
- ❖ fake tongue speakers;
- ❖ fake tongue interpreters;
- ❖ Pastor- Magicians;
- ❖ Pastors who sell handkerchiefs, holi water, calendars, stickers, blessed oil, salt, etc.
- ❖ Pastors who doesn't preach the message on the cross, but prosperity gospel.

These Churches or their pastors may perform signs and wonders, but don't let this persuade you in any way. They are all liars. They claim to be granting the spirit-birth or removing evil spirits whilst in the true sense, they may be strengthening people to become more sinister. This is what the Lord Jesus says about them:

> "Not everyone that says unto me, Lord, Lord, shall enter into the kingdom of heaven; but he that does the will of my Father, which is in heaven."
>
> Matthew 7: 21.

On the Judgment Day, the Lord Jesus shall sit down and command his Angels to bring all the wicked ones who did not "believe" in Him before His judgment seat for the final Judgment. At this time, the fire of hell shall be visible at the left hand of the Lord Jesus.

By visible fire, I mean people will see in the near distance a raging storm of fire which length, breadth and depth cannot be measured. They would see the Angels of God hurling people into it turn-by-turn.

At that time, there shall be no mercy for anyone. Crying shall be useless because tears would be finished from everybody's eyes. Those who will scream shall scream. Those who will wail shall wail, and those who will gnash their teeth, shall gnash their teeth.

On the extreme right hand of the Lord Jesus shall be found the Kingdom of God, which shall also be visible to the wicked ones. They shall see the beauty and the splendor of this mighty city of God and, feel the warmth of blissful life in it. Those going to hell fire shall regret in bitterly and in anguish, but all would be too late.

In one of his powerful lessons, the Lord Jesus showed us this scene in the final day of judgment where He gave the account of Lazarus and a Richman. Both of them lived on earth at the same place, died and went into eternity.

The Lord tells us that Lazarus went to Heaven and the rich man went to hell. The rich man was found tormenting in fierce fire in hell. He then called Lazarus to take a little drop of water with his fingers and drop it on his tongue, but Lazarus told him it was impossible.

In this account, which is a real situation in eternity, the Lord wants to tell His disciples what will happen during the final judgment day. On that fateful day, those who didn't "believe" in the name of the Lord Jesus, and as a result, were not born-again shall tremble and shiver for fear of hellfire which they may see very close by.

They shall be gazing at the Kingdom of God in shame, in anguish and in disgust, but they cannot enter there. Upon seeing their relatives and intimate friends crossing into the Kingdom of Heaven, they shall call on them to give them a drop of water to taste on their tongue, but this shall be impossible.

That time shall be a miserable time because a man may see his beloved wife or child who may wail to him for help, but this man cannot deliver such help. A woman may see her daughter that she loved so much being hurled into the lake of fire. The daughter may try to call the mother, but the plasma between them shall block the call.

This is the picture the Lord Jesus wanted to show humanity for us to know exactly what shall go on during the Day of Judgment. On that fateful day, you shall be able to identify all the people you know and see those going to Hell or those going to Heaven.

At that time, members of mainstream religions, secret spiritual societies, cult groups, and all abominable people shall agree that they deserve hell fire because they refused to "believe" the Lord Jesus when they were on earth.

Those I pity most are false prophets, false apostles, false bishops, self-acclaimed men of God, unfaithful Church elders, deacons, and lukewarm Christians who used the name of Jesus in an unfruitful way.

They had the word "believe" on their lips and mentioned it several times in their lifetime, but did not know it was a concept that was binding on all Christians. These hypocrites would find several excuses for being neglected by the Lord Jesus.

They would struggle with the Lord Jesus in words peradventure upon His kindness, they could be considered for entry into the Kingdom of Heaven. Unfortunately, there shall be no pardon, and there shall be no mercy. They shall be refused entry.

Notwithstanding, greater number of them shall protest vehemently going to hell. They will challenge the Lord Jesus legally that they worked for Him whilst living on earth so He should consider them to enter into the Kingdom of Heaven. Read this for yourself:

> "Many will say to me in that day, Lord, Lord, have we not prophesied in thy name? and in thy name cast out devils? and in thy name done many wonderful works?"
>
> Matthew 7:22.

It shall be more than in the courtroom where people call lawyers to defend them. Over there people shall use all their power, and all their discretion to question the lord. After much questioning, listen to the reply that the Lord Jesus shall give to them:

> "And then will I profess unto them, I never knew you: depart from me, ye that work iniquity."
>
> Matthew 7: 23.

The above scripture means that the Lord Jesus shall sack these people from His presence. These fake pastors and miracle workers that the Lord Jesus shall sack from His presence on the judgment day are the very ones you see today on TV screens, in auditoriums, and Church rooms.

These are the very people you feel so proud of to give you the new-birth when they don't have it themselves. If you claim to be a reasoning being, think about this carefully and decide what to do next.

Don't think that your Church does not entertain fake prophecies, false tongues, and all kinds of sham miracles, and because of that you are in a safe place. You might be in the worst place more than them.

You may also think you are worshiping the Almighty God and obeying the Lord Jesus, with a calm and gentle group like the Jehovah Witness, Mormons, Scientology, the Seventh-day Adventist, the Lutherans and the rest, but I tell you, you may be worshipping and serving Satan.

You may be one of those who chant: "god," "Jesus," "Yah," Yahweh", "YHWH," "Jehovah," "Amen Amen," "Shalom Shalom," "El Shaddai," "Jah," etc., etc. Some of these names can be found in the Bible all right, but they have no roots whatsoever in the Kingdom of God.

Therefore, having these Churches named after biblical words does not guarantee that they are true Christian Churches. If they are not true Churches, then they are false Churches that does not preach the true Christian doctrine.

These churches mention the name of the Lord Jesus, but hate Him the worst of all people. The Jesus' name you hear them calling is not because of any "believe" they have in him, but it's because of your soul which they want for Satan.

They know that half of the world's total population are Christians and that if they do not infiltrate into Christianity, they cannot win souls for Satan. False ministers of Satan are therefore commissioned by agents of Satan to establish pseudo Churches that teach false gospel, which majority of Christians attend these last days.

Some of them distribute free adulterated Bibles, literature, and sometimes relief items for few selected needy persons. They do all these to fascinate weak-minded Christians. Other Churches do everything they can to influence new converts and win them into their evil and willful worship.

The Lord Jesus warns us to be careful of the broad way that leads to destruction. I am also warning you, my cherished readers to be very careful where you worship. Don't be fascinated by Church buildings, interior decorations, member's cars, and the enthusiasm with which members worship in your Church.

Don't be easily influenced by orators and cunning inspirational speakers. Don't be confused with packages of Bible lessons which does not entail the truth. I finally warn you never to remain with them because of the little help they sometimes offer you and other needy members.

Of late, some of the renowned Churches are extorting from members in the form of special offering, payment of tithe, and seed sowing. This has scared and pushed so many people away to join Churches where such monies are not collected.

Cult Churches like the Jehovah witness and the Latter Day Saints would not accept offering or tithe from members. One member of this Church told me the offering he made to the Church the whole year was only one dollar that came from his heart into the offering bowl.

Another person from the Latter Day Saints had told me, "The offering I made in the year are returned to me to use as a startup capital in setting up my own business. Another person from the same Church told me the Church gave him loan to start his own business.

These and many more are some of the things that attract people to such Churches, but I tell you, these Churches are more sinister than some of the Churches that use the name of Jesus to extort monies from members.

Someone may ask me, "Which Church do I attend if all these Churches are sham." You must attend the Church that deeply believes in born-again. Below are few lessons you must expect born-again Churches to teach:

- ❖ Born-again through "believe" in the Lord Jesus alone.
- ❖ The literal second coming of the Lord Jesus to this earth;
- ❖ The soon coming falling away (The one world religion);
- ❖ The Coming of the Antichrist;
- ❖ The resurrection of the dead;
- ❖ Rapture of the Church;
- ❖ The Seven Seals of God;
- ❖ The Seven Trumpets of God;
- ❖ The Seven Vials of God;
- ❖ The Battle of Armageddon;
- ❖ Final Judgment day;
- ❖ Hell and hellfire;
- ❖ The Mystery of the Kingdom of God;
- ❖ The Gospel of Christ;

- ❖ The Kingdom of God.
- ❖ The Christian Talent.
- ❖ The Christian Faith.
- ❖ The Christian Charity.
- ❖ Commandments of the Lord Jesus.

To make assurance double sure, the word of God tells us:

> "Moreover, brethren, I declare unto you the gospel which I preached unto you, which also ye have received, and wherein ye stand; By which also ye are saved, if ye keep in memory what I preached unto you, unless ye have believed in vain. For I delivered unto you first of all that which I also received, how that Christ died for our sins according to the scriptures; And that he was buried, and that he rose again the third day according to the scriptures."
>
> 1 Corinthians 15: 1-4

From the above scripture, we gather that we must attend Churches that teach the death, burial, and resurrection of the Lord Jesus. When you blend this with the guidelines provided above, you'll know the right Church to attend.

You read earlier on that the Jehovah Witness always talk about the "kingdom of god." This is quite different from the Kingdom of God the Lord Jesus came to portray on earth. Man shall rule the Jehovah Witness' "kingdom of god."

According to the Jehovah Witness, the Lord Jesus started ruling in the Kingdom of Heaven in 1914. This implies that He will no longer come down to earth again as He promised His disciples.

I wonder from where they got this date, and which event struck them to make such proclamation?

The true Kingdom of God, which sincere believers cherish, is called "The Kingdom of our God" (Revelation. 12:10). The Kingdom of God hasn't come as yet. It shall be unveiled after the world has been destroyed together with all sinners including the world Satanist elites.

The Lord Jesus, not man, shall rule this kingdom. Therefore, if you are a member of this cult sect and think you are worshipping the Lord Jesus, you deceive yourself. You are serving Satan who has commissioned men to spread lies.

Many other Churches like the Seventh-day Adventist teach end-time programs, which has attracted many followers. I humbly ask you not to admit to their beliefs, which are in variance with the true Christian "believe." They do not believe the born-again that the Lord Jesus taught Nicodemus as well as his entire disciples.

Nicodemus is still at the feet of the Lord Jesus listening attentively with awe and soberness. He's now as cold as ice block and would not dare spread his throat to interrupt the powerful words coming from the Lord Jesus.

The Lord says those who "believe" in him shall be born-again and those who do not "believe" in him shall be condemned. The Lord explains why some people shall be condemned to face eternal hellfire and why others shall inherit eternal life:

> John Chapter 3:19 "And this is the condemnation, that light is come into the world, and men loved darkness rather than light, because their deeds were evil."

This passage means that all those who doesn't believe in the Lord Jesus shall be condemned in Hellfire, and the Lord Jesus has proven the reason for their condemnation. According to the Lord, so many people living today know who He is, and the truth about salvation that He brought to humanity, but they have chosen to belong to different religions.

Jehovah Witness, the Catholic, The Seventh Day Adventist, Mormons, and countless other Christian denominations know all the truth about the Lord Jesus, but have deliberately replaced it with their Church's traditions and lies. They don't believe the born-again which the Lord Jesus taught us to have.

For lack of space, I cannot mention so many Churches here. You will know them by their fruits, and this fruit is their reluctance to openly declare the truth about the born-again concept. I have already given you the clue of how to identify them. The word of God also warns you:

> "That we henceforth be no more children, tossed to and fro, and carried about with every wind of doctrine, by the sleight of men, and cunning craftiness, whereby they lie in wait to deceive"
>
> Ephesians 4:14.

The above scripture is self-explanatory and it's warning every Christian to be careful not to succumb to "every wind of doctrine" (every Church) that are "by the sleight of (cunningly planned by) men" to deceive people. The Word of God continues:

> "But speaking the truth in love, may grow up into him in all things, which is the head, even Christ: From whom the whole body fitly joined together and compacted by that which every joint supplieth, according to the effectual working in the measure of every part, maketh increase of the body unto the edifying of itself in love."
>
> Ephesians 4: 15–16.

The above scripture is simply telling us to put our trust and attend Churches that speak the truth in love. Churches that make members grown in the Lord Jesus. Churches that direct members to look unto only the Lord Jesus for their prosperity, protection and everything in life.

The scripture above did not tell us to attend Churches that occasionally read the Bible making members to love the founder more than the Lord Jesus. Churches that do not mention the name of the founder as if the person is their god.

The Word of God tells us that because people know that God exists, but do not acknowledge Him as God; and because they know what is good, but do not want to do it; God has given them up to reprobate minds to do whatever they want and for that they are without excuse of hellfire. (Romans 1:18–32).

Having said so, the Lord Jesus continues to tell Nicodemus as well as you and the rest of humanity:

> John Chapter 3: 20 "For every one that does evil hate the light, neither comes to the light, lest his deeds should be reproved."

The Lord Jesus says that anyone on earth who shall hesitate to take the free new-birth through simple "believe" in Him as the Son of God loves sin. So many people are unwilling to become born-again simply because they don't know the processes involved.

Most people know the truth, but have ignorantly rejected this truth and gone ahead to burry spiritual pots in their compounds. Others have hidden different idols in secret chambers in their houses upon which they slaughter different domestic animals and sprinkle their blood.

Several others use human parts or kill humans and sprinkle their blood upon their idols. It is no exaggeration to say that several rich men, especially, those from the business community and the ruling class have contracted spirit that pull money for them all the time.

So many people have sold their souls to the devil and have joined one of these Christian cult Churches where they believe they can hide their evil deeds from the public view. Whilst in these Churches, they support every false gospel that comes out from the pulpit.

If you were someone who looks at the outward appearance of people before joining a Church, you would remain in these Churches because of the prominent figures you see there most of whom may be evil people who serve Satan in secrecy.

I have personally met so many people who are not willing to leave their Churches because the President of the nation is a member of their Church. Other people have joined Churches where they see public officials, top artistes and movie stars.

The active membership of such figures have influenced them to refuse making inquiries about the true establishment of these Churches. No matter what you tell these people, they would like to remain the same and to worship with the same Church.

Besides these people are millions and millions of people who attend Churches today, but have denied the powers in the Lord Jesus. Instead to trust God and to "believe" in the Lord Jesus, they have invested all their trust and "believe" in their pastors, apostles and so-called men of God because of the familiar spirits they weird over them.

Some people have turned their pastors to be their fathers and mothers. They respect these sham men of God more than their parents and even the Lord Jesus. Silly married couples have also taken their pastors as their Gods.

Whenever there is a small scuffle between them, instead of settling it themselves, they would carry it to these sham pastors and men of God for settlement. This has resulted in the break-up of several marriages.

The fact is that some of these pastors and ministers of God you adore as gods are trained from top secret societies and are given huge sums of moneys to corrupt the gospel. If you happen to fall in the hands of one of them, they can easily spill your marriage.

I know one top Christian bishop in Accra, Ghana who have divorced the wife in sharp contrast to the true Christian norm and commandment, but who are you to confront this man with this issue. I know the leader of another Church in Accra, Ghana who prefers to be called Angel.

This sham and accursed man of God slept with the wife of his junior pastor and had sex with her. The matter became known and when interviewed on Television, he openly declared; "The holi spirit asked me to do that." He further referred the scripture to what the patriarch David did to the wife of his senior soldier.

This accursed man of God says the Patriarch David couldn't control his lust so he will also continue to sleep with the wives of his junior pastors. If the wives of his own pastors are being treated this way, what shall become of hundreds of beautiful young women who have made him their god. He will likewise sleep with all of them.

Members of some Churches are so deeply hypnotized and mesmerized that whatever you tell them from the Bible about such anomalies doesn't convince them to retreat from such Churches. This is indeed, shocking.

So many modern Churches use moneys collected from evil groups that hate Christianity to build mighty auditoriums, parishes and kingdom halls. It is in such magnificent edifices that the greatest deception and perversion of gospel truth takes place. It is here that many innocent ones who want salvation meet their condemnation in eternity.

The Lord Jesus concludes that those who need salvation and want to enjoy peace and blessings in the Kingdom of God shall never consult sham men of God, idols or spirits for any form of assistance or protection. They shun these abominations and "believe" in the Lord Jesus alone.

The Lord Jesus continues with Nicodemus and say:

> John Chapter 3:21 "But he that does truth comes to the light, that his deeds may be made manifest, that they are wrought in God."

Those who are not interested in sin "believe" in the Lord Jesus and there is no vile in them. They always learn the Bible, observe the commandments of the Lord Jesus, and try to resemble Him in compassion, in humility and in humbleness. These are the born-again Christians.

Nicodemus visited the Lord Jesus at night purposely to inquire about the Kingdom of God and eternal life. When he found out that, the Lord was hammering on what he quested for, he "believed" in the Lord Jesus. This prompted him to keep quiet.

What about you; who profess to be Christian, but have never seated your pastor down and questioned him about eternal life before. There is no time anyone of you asked these pastors how you could enter into the Kingdom of God. Each time you visited them, you carried a burden for prayers.

I am sure by this time you are getting closer to knowing exactly how to become born-again. If so join heads with Nicodemus who will ask no further questions.

> John Chapter 3:22 "After these things Jesus and his disciples came into the land of Judea; and there he stayed with them, and baptized."

The Bible didn't tell us the Lord Jesus came closer to the river Jordan where there was abundant water for Him to baptize. The Bible tells us, He came to the land of Judea and baptized. In this Bible passage, the Word of God is talking about Jesus baptizing with the Spirit, not with water.

This does not necessarily means the Lord Jesus invoked the Holy Spirt to baptize people. What it means is that He taught people how to "believe" in Him and as soon as they did, they became baptized in the Holy Spirit.

Once the Lord has finished teaching Nicodemus, He spiritually baptized him. Not him alone, but as many as believed in His name in the land of Judea to fulfill the spirit baptism He had taught Nicodemus and the world.

I am sure you don't know how to become born-again through "believe" in the name of the Lord Jesus. Don't worry. I'm coming to that very soon so that you can become settled in understanding like Nicodemus who never asked further questions and as a result was baptized in the spirit.

"Believe" is the radical word or concept that has confused so many people and prevented them from becoming born-again. Don't worry, because the Lord Jesus himself will teach you exactly what "believe" is once and for all so that you can become born-again.

12

WHAT IS BELIEVE?

To become born-again one needs to "believe" in the Lord Jesus Christ. "Believe" is a concept within the born-again concept. It is the key word in born-again that we must digest before knowing exactly what born-again means and how to become born-again.

Millions of people attend Churches today and think they "believe" in the Lord Jesus. They mention His name in conversation, use His name in prayers, advise others in the name, sing sweet songs and listen to good news about Him. Because of this, they think they "believe" in the Lord Jesus.

It sounds funny. It seems strange, and I marvel whether they and their pastors do not read the Bible at all. Trust me, if these Christians actually "believed" the Lord Jesus, then I can say that all Christians are born-again and are destined for the Kingdom of God.

On the contrary, if none of them knows what exactly it is to "believe" in the Lord Jesus, then they are all not born-again. It would be by grace alone that some of them would have the opportunity to enter into the Kingdom of God.

I am bold to say this because I have interviewed so many Christians and listened to the teachings of renowned ministers of God, televangelists and Christian scholars. I have also read several books and articles on different internet blocks to make sure what I am saying is not mere exaggeration, but true.

In their sermons, these renowned men of God speak well from the beginning, but when it comes to the point where they should let the actual meaning of born-again or "believe" come out, they shift emphasis.

In every Church you go, the people shout and chant "I believe Jesus" whereas they don't know what it means. In one prayer camp I visited, I asked the members there whether they "believe" in the name of the Lord Jesus.

It was an evening prayer and as soon as this question came from my mouth, tongues speaking broke out to signify that the members that have gathered there were true Christian believers. It wasn't long when a voice sounded; "My Children, I have blessed you. Don't be afraid, because I am with you wherever you are."

What does all these things means? Are they not distortion of truth? How could God's Holy Spirit act and speak this way without meaning? Let me tell you, the Holy Spirt doesn't make useless sounds and noise, but speak wisdom and truth.

"Believe" in the name of the Lord Jesus, is not regular Church attendance, much Bible reading, commitment to one's Church, speaking in tongues, prophesying or singing in the choir. It's something different altogether.

You may know it because I have mentioned it more than twice in this book. Let's now have a look at a practical example of what the Bible calls "believe."

After the ascension of the Lord Jesus, His apostles spread the message about the Kingdom of God.

On one of their evangelical missions, the Apostle Paul and Silas arrived in Philippi, the chief city of Macedonia and stayed there for a while. (Acts 16:12–29).

One day as they went to pray, they met a young unmarried woman possessed with the spirit of divination, which brought her masters much gain by soothsaying. This young woman followed Paul and Silas and cried, saying, "These men are the servants of the Most High God, which shew unto us the way of salvation."

The Apostle Paul, became grieved, and commanded the evil spirit in the young woman to come out of her, and immediately the spirit came out the same hour. This aggrieved the master of the young woman because her soothsaying brought the master many gains.

Being dismayed, the master organized hooligans and caught Paul and Silas, and drew them before the magistrates of the town. Their charge was that Paul and Silas were exceedingly troubling their city, and "teaching different customs that were not lawful for them to teach in a Roman province."

The magistrates tore off their clothes, and commanded Paul and Silas to be beaten. After this, they cast them into prison, charging the jailor to keep them safely. At midnight Paul and Silas prayed, and sang praises unto God so loud that all the other prisoners heard them.

Suddenly! There was a great earthquake which shook the foundations of the prison and immediately all the doors were opened. Their handcuffs and chains got broken. The earthquake awakened the keeper of the prison; and when he saw the cell doors opened, he thought that all the prisoners had run away.

He then decided to commit suicide to avoid embarrassment and harassment by the governor. At this point, the apostle Paul who was sitting calm with Philip cried with a loud voice, saying, "Do thyself no harm: for we are all here."

The Keeper called for a light and conducted a quick check on them to see whether all the prisoners were still in. When he saw that none of them had bolted away, he trembled and fell down before Paul and Silas. At that very moment, he brought Paul and Silas out of the prison cells and asked them:

"Sirs, what must I do to be saved?"

Acts 16: 30.

This question is the same as asking; "What must I do to inherit the Kingdom of God", or "What must I do to get eternal life." Let's digest this question. Firstly, the prison's caretaker was shocked at the occurrence of the earthquake the very night that Paul and Silas were imprisoned.

Secondly, Paul and Silas could have bolted away into their own country after the earthquake, but because they remained in the prison cell, the caretaker believed the message about eternal life, the Kingdom of God, and the born-again that the two preached in that part of the Roman province.

This implies that the counselor "believed" in the message about the Lord Jesus which the two preached earlier on in the day deeply in his heart, compelling him to ask them what he must do in order to be saved. On hearing this from the Caretaker, Paul and Silas said to him:

> "Believe on the Lord Jesus Christ, and thou shalt be saved, and thy house."
>
> Acts 16: 3.

They never asked the prison officer to believe in any particular Church, prophet or man of God, but in the Lord Jesus. They never asked him to bring anointing oil, holy water or money. They never asked him to come and kneel before them so that after they have put their hands on his head and prayed for him, he could get eternal life.

Are you here with me, and do you get this point very clear? All they told him was to "believe" in the Lord Jesus. Let me repeat again! There is nothing again that the two added to "believe" in the Lord Jesus.

Afterwards, Paul and Silas gave the Prison Officer the water baptism to signify that he had become a Christian. This was followed by the Spirit-birth due to the officer's deep conviction about the Lord Jesus and his "believe" in Him.

I have been to a number of Christian crusades and seen how the Churches make new converts. The preacher will tell stories about the Lord Jesus and proclaim that God Almighty lives and is able to solve all problems.

At this point, they will call on those who want to experience the wonderful experience and power of the Lord Jesus to come forward. Others will tell you plainly that if you want prosperity or want your problems solved, you must join them.

After a while, you'll see so many people coming forward to receive Jesus. They come to receive Jesus, but do not come to "believe" in him. I will soon teach you what it is to receive or accept Jesus. This can never be the right approach to making new Christian converts for the Lord.

When the Lord Jesus came, His message was:

> Repent: for the kingdom of heaven is at hand.
>
> Matthew 4:17.

The Lord Jesus came purposely to introduce humanity to the Kingdom of God:

> "And he said unto them, I must preach the kingdom of God to other cities also: for therefore am I sent."
>
> Luke 4: 43.

> "And it came to pass afterward, that he went throughout every city and village, preaching and showing the glad tidings of the kingdom of God: and the twelve were with him."
>
> Luke 8:1.

The Lord Jesus, the founder of Christianity taught His disciples how to evangelize and the message we should carry across. This message was, "Repent for the kingdom of God is at hand." There is nothing more, nothing less.

If during His few days on earth, the Lord Jesus preached repentance and the Kingdom of God, and if the Lord sent His disciples on a preaching practice to preach the message of repentance and the Kingdom of God, why has the message changed these last days?

Why do our Churches invite people to become Christians in order to become prosperous or to overcome problems? This is apostasy. Whenever and wherever I hear a preacher talk much without the core message for winning new converts given us by the Lord Jesus, I see the devil at work.

Wrong Christian Believe

We use believe in our everyday English conversation to mean the trust one have in someone. For example, after telling your children a story, you will ask them whether they believe, and they will response "yes." This is not the believe Christians must have in the Lord Jesus.

When you approach a pastor for prayers, the pastor will ask you to "believe" in the Lord Jesus before the prayer request can be granted. We normally hear pastors ask; "Do you "believe" Jesus can do this or that for you," and the person may respond in the affirmative.

This is also not the "believe" the Lord Jesus says we should have in order to become born-again. The Lord Jesus is talking about "believe" that comes with power from Him. The "believe" that can turn a condemned lost soul into eternal life. Therefore, the Christian "believe" is not the same as the English word "believe."

The True Christian Believe

"Believe" is another Christian concept which has a meaning far different from the believe we use in everyday conversation. Dictionaries have different definition for this Hebrew word. Let's see how the 21st Century dictionary defines the word believe:

- ❖ To accept what is said by someone as true.
- ❖ To accept something said or proposed, e.g. about someone, as true.

Both definitions represent the meaning of the English word believe which we use in our everyday conversation. This is not the same as the "believe" the Lord Jesus told us to have. The Christian "believe" is quite different.

If a person accepts, everything said about the Lord Jesus to be true, it doesn't mean this person believes in the Lord Jesus and for that matter he or she can become born-again. If for instance, you accept that the Lord Jesus was born by the Virgin Mary; or if you accept that Joseph is the father of Jesus, it doesn't constitute "believe" in the Lord Jesus.

You can believe everything said about the Lord Jesus and even say Jesus is the son of God. This is also not "believe" at the Lord's perspective. Therefore, the first definition given by the 21st Century dictionary is in variance with the Christian "believe."

Coming to the second dictionary meaning of the word "believe;" another person may know all the miracles performed by the Lord Jesus; and can enumerate all the ordeals the Lord went through in the hands of the wicked Roman governors and the Israeli elites of his day, but this is not believe in the Lord Jesus that gives eternal life.

Knowing the Bible from cover-to-cover doesn't also constitute believe in the Lord Jesus. You can preach sermon until your listeners begin to cry, and can quote regularly from the Bible to support your message, but this is not believe in the Lord Jesus.

I have a good friend who attends the Synagogue Church of All Nations headed by Pastor T.B. Joshua. This good friend has a twelve-year-old son who can read the first three chapters of the book of John without making mistakes.

Every evening, the entire family gather around the Television set and listen to the channel of the Synagogue Church of all nations that telecast their leader. All the family seems good in the Bible and I can say that my friend is someone who knows the scriptures very well. Unfortunately, for him, he doesn't know what it is to "believe" in the Lord Jesus.

If you go to every university campus, you will meet lecturers, students, and laborers. The laborers see students enter the university and graduating every year, but they themselves are not graduates or cannot become one because they haven't been enrolled as students of the university.

They can continue to work until they have grown old and gone to pension, they will remain laborers. However, there are some exceptional cases where a laborer desirous of getting a higher education would enroll as part-time learner in the university.

It is with so many Christians. They attend Churches all right and hear the word believe, but do not know what it means at the perspective of the Lord Jesus. It's only a few who get the opportunity like laborers who enroll as part-time learners of some universities to become born-again.

Christians who do not know what it is to "believe" in the Lord Jesus behave like two young kids living in a big city whose parents gave them hot water, sugar and cocoa powder to prepare cocoa beverage for their breakfast early in the morning whilst they go to work.

Not knowing exactly what to do, they asked their parents how to prepare the cocoa beverage. The parents instructed them to take spoonful of sugar, milk and cocoa powder and mix in a cup of warm water. The children were happy on hearing this.

Early in the morning, they took a cup of hot water each, gathered the food items at one place and began to recite how to prepare the beverage, 'Daddy and mummy says if we want to prepare cocoa beverage, we should take sugar, milk and cocoa powder and mix in a cup of warm water.'

Does this not sound funny and is it not the same way Christians today treat the concept "believe?" I do not blame anyone because you can search through all dictionaries and encyclopedias, but can't find the true Christian meaning of "believe."

All these dictionaries have explained this Christian concept the way they understand it in English. It's therefore very difficult to know exactly what "believe" is. Without wasting much time again, let's see what "believe" is.

"Believe" is a Hebrew word pronounced, AMAN (וַיְמָאֲהָל). According to Hebrew sources, this word means to be steady, firm and trustworthy. It can also mean to confirm or to affirm. The Bible was first written in Hebrew so I must partly lean upon the Hebrew meaning of the word to make you understand what the Christian word believe means.

According to the Hebrew meaning, the "believe" we must have in the Lord Jesus is to become steady in him and affirm that His words are trustworthy. If a man's words are trustworthy, it is the words he speaks that we check to see whether it is indeed true that he's trustworthy.

Believe therefore is not the story about the Lord Jesus, but by every Word that comes out from His mouth. Any Christian who hears every word that comes out from the Lord Jesus' mouth and agrees to observe them with his or her whole heart, soul and mind, is the one who "believe" in Him.

The emphasis is "The word which comes out from the mouth of the Lord Jesus." If it is the story about Jesus, it is not "believe," but if it is a word that the Lord Jesus has spoken, the moment you take it into your heart and let it become binding upon your life, it is "believe" in Jesus.

Jesus is Lord and God and He came to earth with a particular message. The message is the word from His mouth. That is the reason why we must observe every word that proceeds out from His mouth. Such words are called Testament or covenant of the Lord Jesus.

Let's see one good example of words from the mouth of the Lord Jesus:

> "But I say unto you, That whosoever is angry with his brother without a cause shall be in danger of the judgment: and whosoever shall say to his brother, Raca, shall be in danger of the council: but whosoever shall say, Thou fool, shall be in danger of hell fire."
>
> Matthew 5: 22.

In the above scripture are three testament (covenant or decree by the Lord Jesus). In this covenant or testament, the Lord wants every Christian to do three things, and anyone who does them together with the rest of Jesus' commandments or testaments "believes" in Him.

- ❖ "That whosoever is angry with his brother without a cause shall be in danger of the judgment." Getting angry with a brother can lead to so many bitter consequences including the use of abusive words or killing. This covenant therefore prevents Christians from becoming angry to avoid abusing others or killing which can lead to severe punishment in hellfire.
- ❖ "And whosoever shall say to his brother, Raca, shall be in danger of the council." Raca is a serious insult in Aramaic meaning "useless fellow." If you insult someone this way, you prompt the person to act, which result can lead to chaos. Therefore, the Lord Jesus says if you insult anyone this way

and you are dragged to face the rigorous consequences of the law, it's your own making. Don't blame Christianity.

- ❖ "But whosoever shall say, Thou fool, shall be in danger of hell fire." This is plain language. The moment you say foolish to your neighbor, you stand the danger of going to hell.

The Lord Jesus is Lord and God who has given us this testament (covenant). The moment you read this and agree to put it into practice, you "believe" in the Lord Jesus. The above three decrees from the Lord Jesus together with dozens of others must be binding on all His followers.

You don't just say 'Jesus I believe you' when you do not know the words from His mouth. Each time you hear one of them and you agree to put it into practice, you "believe" in the Lord Jesus. I have a good example of believe which I must briefly share with you.

How To Believe

I was once travelling in a mini-bus with three female students from the Ada University College of Education in Ghana. We were on the first seat. These girls were conversing with each other when suddenly I heard one of them scream, 'You are a fool.'

After this, there was some exchange of words and insults, so I decided to intervene. I stopped them and asked if they were Christians. All of them nodded their heads in response. I again asked whether they respected the Lord Jesus, and they all said "Yes." Finally, I asked them whether they loved Him, and they said "Yes."

I then began by saying: the Lord Jesus told us something in the book of John; "if ye love me, keep my commandments." John 14:15. They agreed. I told them again that one of the commandments of the Lord could be found in Matthew 5: 22 that reads: "But whosoever shall say, Thou fool, shall be in danger of hell fire."

The students became study upon hearing this. I continued that the Bible says we must "let God be true and all men liars." (Romans 3:4). If therefore the words from the mouth of Jesus is true then He means what He says and says what He means. They all agreed to this.

I made it clear to them that once one of them has said to the other 'You fool' she is liable for hellfire according to the decree by the Lord. The girl opened her mouth and told me she didn't know the insult carried such a punishment and that she was sorry.

I told him I am a human who cannot forgive her of any sin except the Lord Jesus. If therefore she had regretted, she should apologize to her friend and ask Jesus for forgiveness. I also told her, once she now knows this testament by the Lord; she should guide her life with it until death.

All three of them closed their eyes in the bus and prayed briefly because the other two knew they had also hurled insults which bitter consequence might carry similar punishment. After that, I took some few minutes to teach them what is born-again and what is the Christian "believe."

The whole event took less than fifteen minutes to finish, but I could see a positive change in the girls. The students grasped the true meaning of "believe" in the Lord Jesus and promised to continue believing in Him.

If these students continue to receive similar teachings from their Churches, they will receive the new-birth. This is what it takes to "believe in the Lord Jesus." The more you study the words from the mouth of the Lord Jesus, the more you "believe" Him, and the more closer you get to born-again.

You cannot believe some words from the mouth of the Lord Jesus and reject some. If you reject any, you don't believe in Him. For example, if you believe some words, but disbelieve the rapture of the Church, you do not believe in the Lord Jesus.

The reason is that we have a vivid account of the rapture from the apostle Paul. Whatever the apostle Paul or any of the Lord's apostles wrote for us in the New Testament were from the Comforter whom the Lord Jesus sent.

Therefore, every testament from the Lord's apostles is also considered the words from the mouth of the Lord Jesus. The moment you agree to keep and practice them, you "believe" the Lord Jesus. If you believe in all the words from Jesus' mouth, but do not believe in judgment day or the glorious literal second coming of the Lord Jesus, you do not "believe" in Him.

So many people attend Church, but do not know anything about the gospel of Christ, the mysteries of the kingdom of God, and the everlasting gospel. There are many who do not know what the Lord Jesus commands us about moral life, marriage, hell and heaven.

Nearly ninety percent of Christians know nothing about the Antichrist, the end time false prophet, and the fundamental Christian concepts and programs of the Lord God. All these people are not born-again and shall end up in hellfire because ignorance is no excuse.

I know you have another stone to throw, but hold on first until this short lesson on "believe" is ended and your bullet had landed on a solid bulletproof metal.

The Jehovah Witness is a cult group, which uses the Bible, but do not believe that the Lord Jesus shall come in person to this world again. They assert that only 144,000 Christians taken from their sect shall enter into the Kingdom of Heaven.

Again, the Lord Jesus commanded us to preach the gospel to the whole world in the name of the Father, The son and the Holy Ghost. (Matthew 28:19). These are the three distinct Gods of Creation who the Bible Calls Godhead (Romans 1:20; Colossians 2:9; Acts 17:29). Christians simply call the Godhead; the Holy Trinity.

The Jehovah Witnesses in their wickedness deny the existence of the Godhead. According to them, the Lord Jesus is not God, but an Angel. They have no basis for this, but no matter where you turn them, they will quote some false scripture to support this unconvincing fable.

These and many more beliefs by this Christian cult prove clearly that they do not "believe" everything that the Lord Jesus taught us. Above all, a staunch Jehovah witness will plainly tell you that he needs not become born-again.

Can we say the Jehovah Witness believe in the Lord Jesus with such dicey teachings and beliefs in the Bible? Some Christian denominations paste the cross of Jesus on a whole wall, and commit members to pray with clapping of hands and stamping of feet from morning to evening every day, whereas this also doesn't qualify them to become born-again or true Christian believers.

Other Christians would roll and summersault like acrobats, but none of these constitutes believe or born-again in the Lord Jesus. After believing in the Lord Jesus, the Christian must move on to having "faith" from where one proceeds finally to "Charity," which are all key Christian concepts needed to become stronger and stronger in the Lord Jesus.

If you are interested to know more about Faith and Charity, please request for my soon coming books entitled:

- ❖ *The Christian Faith; What Is it?*
- ❖ *The Christian Charity; What Is it?*
- ❖ *The Christian Talent; What is It?*

13

ARE WE TO BELIEVE OR TO ACCEPT JESUS AS OUR SAVIOR

The Lord Jesus says, "Believe in me," and receive eternal life. The apostate Christian says; "*accept* Jesus as your personal savior". Which is which? It is expedient to listen to the Lord Jesus than to listen to your pastor or follow the belief and traditions of your Church.

To accept Jesus is different from to "believe" in Him. If someone offers you something, you can refuse or accept it. You can accept a gift today, but may throw it away tomorrow. Many People accepted the Lord Jesus and started going to Churches.

Somewhere along the way, they defected and have now joined different religions. Others are still in the Church, but have denied completely the power in the lord Jesus. As a result, most of them depend upon familiar spirits, and other powers from the devil for their businesses and family protection.

Some Christians become weary of Churches that look dull without any signs and wonders. This pushes them to prayer centers and cult Churches where they think they can get these signs and wonders that does not exist in our days. All these Christians accepted Jesus, but didn't "believe" in Him.

Others truly love the Lord Jesus and have chosen to become Christians. If you love a friend, you will accompany him to any place he asks you to, even if such a place seems dangerous to go. This kind of love is true love. Those who truly love Jesus this way are those who seek a way to "believe" in Him.

Such people defend the truth of the Lord Jesus and stand solidly in their faith even if they should pay with their lives. They love the Lord Jesus with all their hearts, all their souls and all their minds and make sure they act according to His commandments. This is "believe" in the Lord Jesus.

Taking Jesus as our Personal Savior

I have heard several times some Christians asking their friends; 'Have you taken Jesus as your personal savior?' To take Jesus as one's personal savior is the same as to accept Him. You can "take" something now, but may decide to drop it any time.

In the same way, you can take Jesus today, but may decide to drop Him in the near future. So many people took Jesus as their personal savior and have now defected from Christianity to other religions.

We don't "take" Jesus; neither do we "accept" him. Rather, we "believe" in the Lord Jesus. That is what the Lord Jesus commanded us. Therefore, those who enforce you to "accept" or to "take" Jesus as your personal savior are apostate Christians.

14

DO CHRISTIANS NEED RIGHTEOUSNESS OR BORN-AGAIN?

In this chapter, I am coming to deal extensively with righteousness, which so many people claim is the requisite for entry into the Kingdom of God. It is good for one to practice a righteous life, but as far as entry into the Kingdom of God is concerned, this is baseless.

The Lord Jesus commands everyone wishing to enter into the Kingdom of God to be born-again with "Water" and with the "Spirit" through "believe" in Him. These two births is recommended for every Christian including all category of sinners.

Besides this, there is no other way for one to enter into the Kingdom of God. This was the little doubt Nicodemus had during his encounter with the Lord Jesus. He marveled, how unrighteous people could also receive free eternal life through "water" and "spirit" baptism when they haven't practiced any serious pious life before.

Nicodemus, as a proud member of the Pharisee sect read the scripture every day, prayed in the temple two hours day, fasted thrice a week, gave alms regularly to the poor, taught the Mosaic Law and considered these as the certification for eternal life.

This is what the High Priest, the Pharisees, the Sadducees, the Scribes and every Israelite knew was the rightful way to please God. And this was the way they all considered perfect for entry into the Kingdom of God.

In the opinion of Nicodemus, he wondered why the Lord Jesus would not add the "Water" and "Spirit" birth to these existing set of norms and formalities laid down to become righteous. He had every cause to maintain his doubt until the Lord had explained born-again further and further again.

Today, there are different Christian cult groups, which claim to be practicing righteous lives in order to please God. They think they can get the Kingdom of God through righteousness. To them, believe in the Lord Jesus counts nothing.

They are mostly the Old Testament believers. Some of them are strong adherents to the Saturday Sabbath. If it is by self-righteousness that one can please God and to enter into the Kingdom of God, then the Lord Jesus had died in vain.

> "For what saith the scripture? Abraham believed God, and it was counted unto him for righteousness."
>
> Romans 4: 3.

You see clearly in the scripture above that the Lord God doesn't need our righteousness, but "believe." Abraham was called from among the heathen. He wasn't called because of any righteous works. The scriptures now tells us:

> Now to him that worketh is the reward not reckoned of grace, but of debt. But to him that worketh not, but believeth on him that justifieth the ungodly, his faith is counted for righteousness.
>
> Romans 4: 4–5.

Righteousness before God is good, but cannot take anyone into the Kingdom of God. The Bible says, "Obedience is better than sacrifice." The Lord Jesus you claim to follow as your Lord and God says, "believe in me" to become born-again so that you can get eternal life.

Your Church on the other hand says, "Live a righteous life and you shall get eternal life." Why this contradiction, and why are so many Christians following such blind folks? If you will not obey the Lord Jesus, why use His name in your Church.

I know about the African Hebrew Israelites; a small sect that claims to worship God whose founder and leader is Ben Amin. The members of this cult are kind, loving and good in practicing self-righteousness.

I personally know their assistant leader called Nasik Gavriel who is deeply committed to the Old Testament Bible. I quite remember the day he sat me down in his Hall, opened his Bible and quoted from Exodus 23:13, which reads:

> "And in all things that I have said unto you be circumspect: and make no mention of the name of other gods, neither let it be heard out of thy mouth."

He quoted this to draw my attention to the fact that the names of days, and months were all named after idols and that it was not good for one to mention these names. This implies that the African Hebrew Israelite would never say for example, Monday, Tuesday, January, or March.

Instead, they would say, the second day of the week, the third day of the week, the first month, the second month etc. They know that if they ever mentioned these names, they could contravene this commandment of the Lord God.

Besides this, members of this cult group practice righteous lives that in their eyes is pleasing to God. They think it's a command from God for every human seeking for him to be righteous. This is quiet true, but one thing we must know is that the Mosaic laws came with ordinances, which the Lord God asked the people to observe as well.

> "Ye shall do my judgments, and keep mine ordinances, to walk therein: I am the LORD your God."
>
> Leviticus 18: 4.

In the ancient days, when one committed any sin, the person was asked to make sacrifice of, goats, guinea fowls, dove, bullocks, lambs, he goats," etc. Other sacrifices were burnt offerings, burning of incense, candles, etc., to pacify God. This is what the Bible calls "Ordinances of God."

It is good for Christians to observe the commandments of the Lord, but for its related ordinances. Why am I saying so? Under the ordinances, as soon as one commits any sin, the person would carry the requisite sacrifice to the temple and ask for forgiveness. The ordinances gave the people the license to commit more sins.

Because of the ordinances, the nation Israel became polluted with sins to an unbearable point. God's people never respected the laws, neither the ordinances. They altered both the laws and the ordinances to suit their evil ends. The Lord God saw this and declared through the prophet Isaiah:

> "The earth also is defiled under the inhabitants thereof; because they have transgressed the laws, changed the ordinance, broken the everlasting covenant."
>
> Isaiah 24:5

Filled with the Spirit, the prophet Zachariah also declared:

> "Yea, they made their hearts as an adamant stone, lest they should hear the law, and the words which the LORD of hosts hath sent in his spirit by the former prophets: therefore came a great wrath from the LORD of hosts."
>
> Zachariah 7: 12.

The Lord God saw the fast rate at which the people sinned because of the ordinances and declared through the prophet Isaiah:

> "To what purpose is the multitude of your sacrifices unto me? saith the LORD: I am full of the burnt offerings of rams, and the fat of fed beasts; and I delight not in the blood of bullocks, or of lambs, or of he goats."
>
> Isaiah 1: 11.

The Lord God continued in His protests:

> "Bring no more vain oblations; incense is an abomination unto me; the new moons and sabbaths, the calling of assemblies, I cannot away with; it is iniquity, even the solemn meeting."
>
> Isaiah 1: 13.

From the above scripture quotes, we see clearly that the Lord God was fed up with the proliferation of sins. He was no longer interested in sacrifices that the people offered to atone for their sins. The Lord God also declared as iniquity all observances associated with the new moons and the Sabbath day.

The Lord God also gave the nation Israel certain feast to observe. These included the feast of Passover and the feast of Unleavened Bread, (Read Leviticus 23: 4–6). The people used these occasions to cause abominations unto the Lord. The Lord God again became fed up with these feasts and declared:

> "Your new moons and your appointed feasts my soul hateth: they are a trouble unto me; I am weary to bear them."
>
> Isaiah 1: 14.

The Lord God saw that the people needed a new set of commandments that contained no observances. The word of God tells us:

> "Therefore by the deeds of the law there shall no flesh be justified in his sight: for by the law is the knowledge of sin.
>
> Romans 3: 20.

The scripture above has summarized it all that no man can be justified before God through the old commandants and its related ordinances. After the Lord Jesus has come, Christians need no law to justify them. We don't need those burn offerings, and sacrifices again.

We need the righteousness of the Lord Jesus, which are enshrined in His commandments written in the New Testament. The Book of Galatians throws a bright light upon this:

> "Knowing that a man is not justified by the works of the law, but by the faith of Jesus Christ, even we have believed in Jesus Christ, that we might be justified by the faith of Christ, and not by the works of the law: for by the works of the law shall no flesh be justified."
>
> Galatians 2: 16.

The Lord Jesus has given Christians a new commandment, which is called the Testament of the Lord Jesus, which we must observe. Those who admit to this and observe them are the very people who "believe" in the Lord Jesus.

On the other hand, those who reject the commandments are those that the Lord Jesus says shall go into eternal condemnation. In sum, Christians are no longer under the Mosaic Law and its related ordinances. We are under the Testament of the Lord Jesus.

Nasik Gavriel, my good friend; the African Hebrew Israelite, worships and loves God. Unfortunately, he sees the Lord Jesus as one of the great prophets of the Bible, but does not "believe" in Him as a savior of the world.

During the short time of our friendship, I was someone who loved God, but wasn't a sincere Christian. He saw my deep love for the Lord God and wanted to win me into this sect at a time when I was wandering in opinion regarding which true Church to attend.

He gave me so many study materials and the sect's absorption manual to read before taking their baptism. This came with the promise that they will take me to their headquarters in Israel. After my return, they will make me the administrator of their Soya factory in Tema, Ghana.

After glancing through their absorption manual, I saw a great difference between this and what the Bible actually says about baptism. By the grace of God, I refused the baptism and escaped from death to the amazing grace that I enjoy with the Lord Jesus today. Thank you Jesus!

This is what every Christian must do. Don't just join any Church without first knowing their basic beliefs.

The Church called "Shallom Shallom," the Seventh-day Adventist and all Sabbath keepers believe in the Old Testament commandments and rejects the irrefutable facts of the New Testament that enjoins us to observe the commandments of the Lord Jesus in order to become born-again.

All these groups claim to be Christian Churches, but to them, "believe" in Jesus Christ for the new-birth sounds nonsense. They are lost because they do not know the value of the Christian concept born-again. I cannot leave this matter to lie without referring these cult sects to the truthful Words of God:

> "But before faith came, we were kept under the law, shut up unto the faith which should afterwards be revealed."
>
> Galatians 3: 23.

The Bible quote above is telling us that before the coming of the Lord Jesus, the Israelites and the entire world was unquestionably under the law. Now that the Lord Jesus has come, no one is under this law again. The Word of God explains why:

> "Wherefore the law was our schoolmaster to bring us unto Christ, that we might be justified by faith. But after that faith is come, we are no longer under a schoolmaster."
>
> Galatians 3: 24–25

I wonder whether these Sabbath keepers do not read scriptures like this. I am sure they do, but for distortion of the gospel's sake, they stick to this old system. This is done to deceive their ignorant members who aren't willing to learn scriptures apart from the booklets and study materials supplied them by the Church.

If you're a member of any of these sects, listen to what the Word of God is telling you:

> "For ye are all the children of God by faith in Christ Jesus. For as many of you as have been baptized into Christ have put on Christ."
>
> Galatians 3:26–27.

The scripture above is simply telling us that the Lord God in the days of the ancient Israelites counted His beloved children by those who observed the Mosaic laws. Today however, because the Lord Jesus has come, we become the children of God by putting (believing) on Christ. To put on Christ or believing in Christ is to become born-again.

After the coming of the Lord Jesus, the Almighty God doesn't know the people of Israel only as His people. The people of the Lord God are those who "believe" in the Lord Jesus. Such people are the ascendants of Abraham and are called the Saints of the Lord Jesus. The Word of God explains this further:

> "There is neither Jew nor Greek, there is neither bond nor free, there is neither male nor female: for ye are all one in Christ Jesus. And if ye be Christ's, then are ye Abraham's seed, and heirs according to the promise."
>
> Galatians 3: 28–29.

15

WORKS AND BORN-AGAIN

Those who follow righteousness and think they can please God through this are those who stick to works. They adhere strongly to fasting, prayers, and abstention from evil deeds. That's fine. Others go further to obey the Ten Commandments to the letter.

These indeed are good qualities for moral life, but the Lord Jesus didn't ask us to be practicing any work before we could become born-again. If this is what you believe in, you shall be judged according to your works.

In the olden days, when the nation Israel was wandering in the wilderness, the Lord God asked them to look at the brass snake hanged on the tree in order to be saved from death caused by dangerous snakebites.

As soon as the one bitten by snake looked, up and saw the brass snake that was hanged on a tree, the person recovered instantly from the snakebite. The healing came as a result of believe on the part of the snake bitten victim.

In our modern times, the Lord Jesus asks us to "believe" in His name in order to become righteous, and have eternal life. According to Him, this can grant us to see and to enter into the Kingdom of God.

There is no need for doubt here. One of the criminals who hanged on the cross with the Lord Jesus Christ who had no slightest "believe" in the Lord Jesus yelled:

> "If thou be Christ, save thyself and us."
>
> Luke 23: 39.

According to the Bible account, the other criminal who saw no vile in the Lord Jesus, rebuked his counterpart who made that blasphemous statement by saying:

> "Dost not thou fear God, seeing thou art in the same condemnation? And we indeed justly; for we receive the due reward of our deeds: but this man hath done nothing amiss."
>
> Luke 23:40, 41.

Although this notorious criminal had done no righteous works neither had he followed any steps to righteousness yet he has expressed the sentiment of "believe" in the Lord Jesus. In his rebuke statement, he declared that Jesus was God when he said, "Dost not thou fear God)."

I can testify that for such statement to have come out from the mouth of a dying criminal in defense of the Lord Jesus was an expression of strong "believe" in the Lord Jesus which supersedes all "believes."

This criminal might be someone who knew the Lord Jesus very well, but would not have the time to follow or worship Him. He could be one of the unemployed youth who survived life through armed robbery.

Though he was not one of the disciples, yet he knew the Lord Jesus to be God. He might have heard all what the people said about him, but to stop stealing and follow the Lord was his problem. He knew without doubt that the Lord Jesus came to proclaim the Kingdom of God and to show how people could enter into it.

He might have heard about Nicodemus' encounter with the Lord Jesus and how the news spread like a brushfire that a certain man called Jesus, considered to be God on earth has made a decree known as born-again that qualifies his sincere followers for entry into the Kingdom of God.

If this was his assertion, then when he saw the Lord Jesus also hanged on the cross with him, he became amazed and worried. He could see that his crucifixion was because of envies on the part of the High Priest and the Israeli governing council.

At this last moment of his life when he was cogitating about these things, he was also contemplating about eternal life, which he might have heard in the air that it can come after one is born-again.

He might have cast his mind on the fact that the Lord Jesus could forgive sins and that He had on several occasions forgiven so many people their sins. He had also heard about spirit-birth that was given to people who have neither worked nor followed any acts of righteousness.

Finally, he also believed that it was only the Lord Jesus who granted this spirit-birth. Therefore, by gathering his last strength, he yelled:

"Remember me when thou comest into thy kingdom."

Luke 23: 42.

This is to me; a shocking statement I would ever expect from a dying criminal. No dying criminal will ever call on other dying criminal suffering equal pains with him to save him had it not been due to his deep "believe" in such a person.

The criminal highly estimated the Lord Jesus to be God who was fulfilling a specific mission for humanity on earth for that matter; he didn't call on anyone, not even the closest soldier to save him, but the Lord Jesus.

Sometimes when I think about this criminal, I wonder why he didn't devote that short time of his last breathe to thinking about the wickedness of his murderers who hanged him, but rather thinking about the Lord Jesus and trying to defend Him.

In these last days, only a few Christians would be able to make such pronouncement on their sick beds and at the point of death when all hopes are gone. I know only a few Christians would stand firm for the Lord Jesus when their businesses start to collapse.

I am sure only a few Christians can withstand the loss of loved ones. Only a few still can remain strong in their faith when it comes to dying for the Lord Jesus. The simple reason is that so many Christians do not "believe" in the Lord Jesus and are not born-again.

When troubles come upon Christians, instead of putting their trust in the Lord Jesus, they rather blame him and shift their trust to false prophets and sham men of God. The Lord Jesus knows our problems and calls them "Heavy Laden."

The Lord knows that we are humans who oftentimes fall into problems. He therefore promised rest to all Christians who carry such problems:

> "Come unto me, all ye that labour and are heavy laden, and I will give you rest."
>
> Matthew 11: 28.

This is a positive command from the Lord Jesus to all those who need help. The Lord says we should come to Him personally in prayers for answers to our problems. Because we do not "believe" in him, we turn to quack pastors, prophets, apostles and self-acclaimed men of God for solutions that never come.

Christians today want quick answers to their problems. The Lord Jesus has such quick answers, but for lack of patience, (That is disregard for another important commandment of the Lord), Christians rush to different sham men of God who invokes familiar spirit upon them.

Others will deny all trust in the Lord Jesus and go to the fetish shrine for assistance to resuscitate their businesses and for family protection. As they do this, they may be staunch members of a renowned Church. This is hypocrisy!

One most funny thing I see about all Churches and their members is that they have shifted their attention from the Words of the Lord to prayers these last days. It is good to pray always, but the Lord Jesus never asked us to pray in order to become born-again.

He told us to "believe in him." This is what the apostles also taught us and this is what all die-hard Christians know. I hear many Christians say, "I am tired of praying." Indeed, you will become tired of prayers.

What prompted them to say this? How can prayers receive quick and good response when the person doesn't "believe" in the Lord Jesus? Take it from me that a Christian's prayer becomes more effective only when the person "believes" in the name of the Lord Jesus.

The man on the cross besides the Lord Jesus is a notorious criminal, who knew that the Lord Jesus would not be able to rescue him from the physical death ahead of him. Notwithstanding, he looked beyond this physical existence and entrusted his eternity into the care of the lord Jesus who he saw as God.

He did not look down upon the Lord as most of us do today. He was aware that the Lord Jesus predicted His own death on the cross. He gathered this information from the Lord's conversation with Nicodemus. Whilst still on the cross, he memorized the Lord's saying:

> "And I, if I be lifted up from the earth, will draw all men unto me."
>
> John 12: 32.

The Lord Jesus who knows the thought of every man was sternly gazing at the criminal spiritually to discern his thoughts. The statement of believe made by the criminal touched his heart whilst still on the cross. He sees how deeply a dying criminal believes in him. He sees how a dying criminal quests for salvation.

Although the Lord Jesus looked restless with pains from severe torture, the criminal saw Him as spiritually strong to forgive him of his sins and to save him from eternal condemnation. Immediately the Lord Jesus replied the criminal:

> "And Jesus said unto him, Verily I say unto thee, To day shalt thou be with me in paradise."
>
> Luke 23: 43.

The Lord Jesus on His part has granted the criminal eternal life to fulfill the fact that He's the only one assigned in both Heaven and earth to grant eternal life. Again He's done this to testify that entry into the kingdom of God doesn't require righteousness or works, but "believe" in Him.

The usage of Paradise appears only thrice in the Bible. 2 Corinthians 12:4; Revelation 2:7 and Luke 23:43. The Lord Jesus says Paradise is the place His Saints go immediately after death, and to be with the Lord Jesus wherever He might be in eternity meant that the criminal became born-again.

You can see that the new-birth can come at any time in one's lifetime after believing in the Lord Jesus, and it comes only at the discretion of the Lord Jesus. The Lord Jesus says the criminal shall be with him in Paradise, and I have already explained to you what paradise is.

There is no need for any useless argument on what and where paradise is. These apostate Christians have given so many false information about paradise in books and on the internet that I won't waste time to share with you.

Dear reader, if you have also "believed" in the Lord Jesus the same way as this criminal, though you are on a dead bed and thinking all hopes are gone, you shall receive the new-birth to get the Kingdom of God.

The criminal's encounter with the Lord Jesus and other similar encounters where people had received eternal life after "believing" in the name of the Lord Jesus, affirm the fact that the Lord Jesus didn't command anyone to seek for work, but to seek for "believe" in him in order to become born-again.

Many Christian denominations ask new members to practice works, which include constant prayers, attending regular Church meetings and services, weeding and cleaning Church premises, etc. What does all these things means?

Other Churches compel members to pay accurate tithe, regular dues, huge offerings, and tell them to shun evil doing so that the Lord Jesus can give them the new-birth. Unknowingly, the more they do these things, the farther away they shift from born-again, and the closer they get to their graves without becoming born-again.

The Church of Pentecost would ask members to pray constantly until the spirit of God gives the new convert the utterance to speak in tongues, they can't be born-again. Where from this allegory? Is this not an indictment on this so-called spirit-filled church?

The Church of Christ, the Church of God and several others would ask new converts to stop smoking, drinking, fornication, and all forms of sins before they could become born again. I wonder whether they do not read the Bible.

Nicodemus was a member of the Pharisee sect who contended against the truth of the Lord Jesus. When he was being taught the born-again concept, the Lord Jesus did not ask him to stop sinning. The apostle Paul was once persecuting the disciples of the early Church.

He wasn't asked by the Lord God to stop persecuting the disciples before the Lord Jesus called him. He was called while he was still in his sins. Any Church that teaches members to stop sinning before they can receive the new-birth is satanic Church.

These days, some Churches doesn't ask members to become born-again, all they do is inviting the spirit to the Church and suddenly, the people shall start screaming and making useless sounds as if they are mad.

Why take a wrong way to your house when there is a shorter and perfect one to pass? I am not telling you to avoid your long prayers, the strange tongues, all-night attendance, tithe payments and the other stuffs.

What I mean is that you must "believe" in the Lord Jesus Christ side-by-side with these works of the flesh. When you become born-again, you shall stop most of these things that are repugnant to the Lord Jesus.

After you are born-again, the entire roaming, meandering, summersaulting, screaming, barking, rolling and noise making shall all cease. After you become born-again, you will laugh at all these sycophancy.

16

THE LORD JESUS TEACHES HIS DISCIPLES WHAT IT IS TO WORK FOR GOD

In the previous pages, I tried to explain what it takes to "believe" in the Lord Jesus, but did not get to the details. I know you are still lost because of this. Don't worry at all, because I would like the Lord Jesus himself to tell you what it is to "believe" in him.

On the cross of Calvary, the Lord Jesus shouted; "I have finished." This was the proof that He gave to humanity whatever information you and I needed to become reconciled to the Lord God. In other words, He has given us every detailed information regarding eternal life and entry into the Kingdom of God.

The Lord says we must be born-again. He adds that this could be done when we "believe" in Him. "Believe" is the hallmark of the New Testament Bible. This word is found floating virtually in every page of the New Testament signifying its importance to the Christian seeking to enter into the Kingdom of God.

If the Lord Jesus did finish his work, then it means that He did not leave us in suspense regarding what "believe" in His name means. If you are ready to know the final meaning of "believe" then discard every information, you have about it and let the Lord teach you.

The nation Israel believed in the Ten Commandments and set of laws given them by the Lord God. They observe these commandments and laws with the idea of getting the Kingdom of God after death.

Here comes the Lord Jesus on the scene who teaches a different entry condition into the Kingdom of God that the people had never heard before. During His earthly ministry, many people followed the Lord Jesus wherever He went.

They all knew that every man born to this earth must do something to please the Lord God. They also heard the Lord Jesus say several times, "I must do the will of my father who sent me." If the Lord Jesus does the will of the father on earth, it means He works for God.

His followers also wanted to know what to do to work for God. This prompted the disciples one fateful day to ask the Lord Jesus:

> "What shall we do, that we might work the works of God?"

> John 6: 28.

In simple language, the followers of the Lord Jesus wanted to know what they must do in order to please God to qualify them for entry into the Kingdom of God. Should they continue keeping the Mosaic Law together with its ordinances?

Should they fast thrice a week, offer lengthy prayers two hours daily in the temple, or pay their tithe in full. Again, they wanted to know whether they should strengthen their routine burnt offerings, and other sacrifices.

If these are not the way, should they stop all forms of sins, make pastor's their gods, wash their cars, their clothes, give them the best of gifts from their hearts, or what is it actually to work for God? This important question needs an answer from the Lord Jesus.

I see this as another wise question that could only come from the disciples of the Lord Jesus. They could ask such a wise question because they were close to Him and wanted to understand the born-again concept very well.

The answer the Lord Jesus gave the disciples can settle all arguments and misconceptions surrounding the Christian concept "Believe." Don't forget that the disciples in question were all Jews who were strong adherents to the Mosaic law.

Thinking that the answer from the Lord Jesus was going to strengthen their old system of belief, it turned the other way round. The Lord Jesus explained to them what "believe" is and its link with the born-again concept. This is the answer:

> "Jesus answered and said unto them, This is the work of God, that ye believe on him whom he hath sent."
>
> John 6: 29.

The answer "Believe" on him whom he hath sent" is the only correct answer not the lengthy works of the flesh, or righteousness. The statement "Believe" on him whom he hath sent" refers to the Lord Jesus Christ himself.

We must believe in the Lord Jesus. The moment we do this as Christians, we work the work of God. Even today, two thousand years after the Lord has explained this, pastors teach that we must spread the gospel, and do certain things before we can do the work of God. The Lord Jesus didn't teach us this.

If you take "believe" in the scripture above to mean a simple trust in Jesus, it means Christians don't know what they are doing as the children of God. How can you trust in Jesus only, and claim you are working for God?

The answer the Lord Jesus gave to His disciples once again proves that indeed, born-again is an entry visa into the Kingdom of God. "Believe" is the master, and "works," or "righteousness" are the servants. If the master praises, what are servants.

The Apostle Peter, leader of the twelve Apostles, affirms that the new-birth does not depend upon works, the righteousness of a person or, simply by putting away one's filth of the flesh. It is through the "believe" that the Lord Jesus died and resurrected:

> "The like figure whereunto even baptism doth also now save us (not the putting away of the filth of the flesh, but the answer of a good conscience toward God,) by the resurrection of Jesus Christ."
>
> 1 Peter 3: 21.

The apostle is talking about "believe" in the Lord Jesus. According to him, this can save the Christian and give him eternal life. He didn't talk about righteous life. He further added that we must have a good conscience towards God having resurrected the Lord Jesus Christ.

If it is believing in the Lord Jesus that gives us the new-birth, then we can say it is by grace of God. Without grace, all of us might have been lost: The Apostle Paul summarizes it in this golden verse:

> "For by grace are ye saved through faith; and that not of yourselves: it is the gift of God: Not of works, lest any man should boast."
>
> Ephesians 2:8–9.

I will come back to the answer the Lord Jesus gave His disciples when they asked Him to tell them what they must do to do the work of God. After the explanation, you will feel settled in understanding. However, before I do, let's see how water and the spirit baptism take place first.

17

HOW WATER BAPTISM TAKES PLACE

The actual water baptism recommended by the Lord Jesus is immersion into water to signify the burial of the convert's body and the washing away of his or her sins. A pastor or any Christian believer can do water baptism in flowing rivers and streams.

Some Churches choose to baptize new converts by sprinkling water upon them due to non-availability of rivers and streams in their locality. This doesn't contradict anything in Christianity once you know the true meaning of what water baptism is.

Water-birth is the proclamation by the new Christian convert that he or she agrees to the fact that he or she is a sinner who needs pardon from the Lord Jesus. It is also the confirmation that once your sins are forgiven, you will lead a clean life devoid of sins. The Word of God explains further:

> "Knowing this, that our old man is crucified with him, that the body of sin might be destroyed, that henceforth we should not serve sin."
>
> Romans 6: 6.

You see that the new convert who accepts to take the water baptism must agree that he or she will never go back to the former life in the world. For the new Christian convert to accept the water baptism means that he or she shall lead a Christian life from the time of his or her baptism till death.

If you have any other views apart from what the Bible quote above has told you, it implies you need no water baptism, or you aren't ready for water baptism. The Word of God explains this in details:

> "But he that lacketh these things is blind, and cannot see afar off, and hath forgotten that he was purged from his old sins."
>
> 2 Peter 1: 9.

According to the scripture above, before and after you receive the water baptism, you must make up your mind to come out from your old bad ways for the new ways in the Lord Jesus to take control over your life. If you lack this truth, you're blind.

As soon as you receive the water birth, the Bible tells us you have signed an agreement with the Lord Jesus. This agreement is that you shall follow the Lord Jesus the rest of your life. The other side of the agreement is that the Lord Jesus pardons you of all your sins.

> "Therefore, if any man be in Christ, he is a new creature: old things are passed away; behold, all things are become new."
>
> 2 Corinthians 5: 17.

The above scripture quotes mean that after becoming a Christian:

- ❖ If at first you smoke cigarette, drunk alcohol and abused narcotic drugs, you must stop.
- ❖ If at first you fornicated with girls for affection, you must stop.
- ❖ If at first you fornicated with men for money, you must stop.
- ❖ If at first you fornicated behind your husband or wife, you must stop.
- ❖ If at first you worshipped idols, you must stop.
- ❖ If at first you worshipped saints, angels or other powers, you must stop.
- ❖ If at first you were a thief, or a fraudster, you must stop.
- ❖ If at first you used powers from a pastor or a fetish priest to sell, you must stop.
- ❖ If at first you corrupted the gospel of the Lord Jesus, you must stop.
- ❖ If at first you followed false prophets and false christs, you must stop.

All these are worldly things. The Word of God warns us to avoid doing these things. After water baptism, we must guide our movement, speech and every action we are about to take with one question;

"Shall the Lord be pleased if He were standing close to me and sees me doing this?"

After the water baptism, we may be susceptible to sin. The new believer needs to exercise self-control in order to avoid going back to sin. You may be controlled by your old sinful nature until the Lord grants you the second birth, which is the Spirit birth.

This implies that after the water baptism, we must strive hard for the Spirit baptism.

> "For they that are after the flesh do mind the things of the flesh; but they that are after the Spirit the things of the Spirit. So then they that are in the flesh cannot please God"

Romans 8:5, 8.

According to the scripture we just read, the water birth alone doesn't make one the son of God. It neither qualifies one into the Kingdom of God.

18

HOW SPIRIT BAPTISM TAKES PLACE

In this chapter, I will finalize the explanation of what it is to "believe" in the Lord Jesus to settle all arguments so that you do not continue to live as a Christian for several years of your life without becoming born-again.

After one is baptized by water, he again needs the spirit-birth, which comes about, because of one's "believe" in the Lord Jesus:

> "He that believeth and is baptized shall be saved; but he that believeth not shall be damned."
>
> Mark 16: 16.

This type of baptism leads into eternal life. Without the spirit-birth, one can never become born-again. Anyone on earth who doesn't receive this Spirit baptism shall be condemned into eternal hellfire.

Every Christian may want to receive the Spirit birth, but to know how and where to receive it had always been the problem. This is where quack men of God get the weak-minded Christians. There are several ways false Churches use today to grant the Spirit birth contrary to what the Bible has taught us.

I quite remember one incident when I was a child of twelve. My elder sister took me to a Church where the pastor always asked members to repeat the name "Jesus" several times and as much as one can, during prayer time.

The motive behind this prayer was for everyone to receive the spirit-birth. This was the first prayer during every Church service, which was done for about fifteen minutes. After the break, there is a short Bible reading before the rest of the prayers continue.

At such a young age, I didn't know the meaning and significance of spirit-birth neither salvation nor eternal life. All I knew was to listen to the prophet who urged all of us to become spiritually born-again.

To receive the spirit-birth, he will urge every new member to prepare to shout at the top of their voices in order to attract the attention of the Lord Jesus.

The wonderful thing I saw about this prayer was that within these few minutes, the holi spirit shall descend and suddenly, you will hear people screaming, shouting and making all sorts of futile noise.

What I used to do was that I always joined these members to repeat "Jesus," "Jesus," "Jesus," in a non-serious manner every day until the bell rang for the next prayer. I wasn't lucky one day. I was jokingly chanting the name when suddenly the bell rang for us to stop. This was the time when we were about only six minutes into prayers.

Instead for me to stop as usual, I did not stop. I continued chanting; thinking that the next prayers would continue as usual. Suddenly I heard the late Prophet *Abene* telling the entire congregation to sit down. I was still chanting the name in a frenzy manner.

I heard the pastor telling the congregation to look at me. He then continued; 'This boy came to the Church just some few weeks ago, but has received the Holy Spirit baptism.' 'Most of you are not serious of the spirit-birth, and for that matter, you cannot get it.' He continued.

I heard this clear and loud, and felt very shy. I intentionally closed my eyes and continued shouting without knowing how to end the chanting. This created the impression that I had truly receive the spirit-birth.

Chanting "Jesus, Jesus, Jesus" continuously for about twelve minutes wasn't a small task for a boy of my age. I continued for about ten minutes and became tired. I then decided to end the drama by going outside the Church room.

When I got out, the prophet and his pastors followed me to a fountain, which was very close to the Church building. I began drinking from the waters of the fountain and this ended it all. This short episode became the talk of the day that particular Sunday.

The prophet said emphatically that I had received the spirit-birth whereas I knew within myself that I had not received any spirit baptism. The more he made mention of this, the more I resisted in my mind.

Since from the beginning of this book, I have been hammering on spirit baptism several times, but haven't touched on how it takes place. Anyway, it can take place only by believing in the name of Lord Jesus. At this point, I will let John the Baptist, the forerunner of the Lord Jesus to speak.

He is the gospel potentate, and the prophet-mediator between the Old Testament prophets of God and the New Testament Lord Jesus and His apostles. I will let him tell us how one can receive the spirit birth:

> "I indeed baptize you with water unto repentance: but he that comes after me is mightier than I, whose shoes I am not worthy to untie: HE SHALL BAPTIZE YOU WITH THE HOLY GHOST, AND WITH FIRE."
>
> Matthew 3: 11.

John the Baptist came to open the way to the beginning of the Lord's ministry. He came baptizing people with water, which according to him was for repentance of sins. He then hinted us about another baptism which he said was the Spirit baptism.

According to John someone mightier than him was coming to grant people the Spirit baptism. We all know that John the Baptist came to testify about the Lord Jesus. The one mightier than him whose shoes he was not worthy to untie is the Lord Jesus. I hope this is very clear. Having concluded so let's quickly shift to the spirit-birth.

Getting the spirit-birth is what has confused many people for centuries; but today is today. The truth shall come out as the Lord Jesus himself is ready to teach you this controversial subject and not any other person.

Let's quickly take a powerful statement from the Lord Jesus on how He baptizes those who believe in his name with the Holy Ghost and with fire. We take this short scripture from the book of John Chapter 6 verse 33:

> Chapter 6:33a "It is the spirit that quickeneth; the flesh profiteth nothing."

The above scripture quote is telling us that the Spirit baptism stimulates us to become active in the Lord Jesus, but as for the flesh or water baptism, it doesn't help us to become active in the Lord Jesus.

From this point, let's continue with the rest of the Bible quote, and see how the Lord Jesus gives the Spirit birth:

> Chapter 6:33b "The words that I speak unto you, they are spirit, and they are life."

Glory be to the Lord Jesus who teaches us His truth to enable us grow in Him every day and to become born-again. He is our "Lord and our God," the "Word of God," the "Alpha and Omega," "King of Kings and Lord of Lords." Thanks be to His name. The answer has finally come out from the Lord's own mouth.

Our Lord and our God who do not want anybody to perish has shown us the way to pass in order to "believe" in his name so that we can receive the Holy Spirit baptism. Let us read His statement again:

> "The words that I speak unto you, they are spirit, and they are life."

The Lord Jesus says that the Words He speaks from his mouth is 'spirit' and 'life.' He didn't say the stories written about Him. The Lord Jesus who is supreme physicists is speaking physics language here. In electricity, the 'life' wire is the one, which contains 'fire.'

"Life" in the scripture context therefore means the same as "fire" which John the Baptist used. The usage of "Spirit" is also the same as the Holy Ghost. Therefore, if you replace 'life' in the scripture above with 'fire' the statement from the Lord will read:

> "The words that I speak unto you, they are spirit, and they are fire."

This is not different from what John the Baptist also said, "HE SHALL BAPTIZE YOU WITH THE HOLY GHOST, AND WITH FIRE." The Holy Ghost is the same as the Spirt. We see a perfect synchronization of scripture here. Once again let's see how we can receive the spirit-birth from the Lord Jesus' own mouth:

> "The words that I speak unto you, they are spirit, and they are life."

John 6:33b

What are the words from the mouth of the Lord Jesus? These are His testament, or commandments or the instructions, or the warning, or the details He gave us about the Godhead, about creation, about human's sinful nature, about the Kingdom of God, about eternal life, about the forgiveness of sin, about hell, about judgment day, about marriage, about moral life, etc., etc.

Now let's come to fire or the spirit-birth. In a common parlance, if fire did not destroy, it does well for us. This type of fire that the Lord Jesus is talking about burns our infirmities and filth and purges us.

The moment you hear these instructions, or commandments, or testament from the mouth of the Lord Jesus and determine in your heart to observe them, you "believe" in the name of the Lord Jesus.

At the discretion of the Lord Jesus, He sends the Holy Ghost to burn all your old nature and infirmities and grants you the sprit-birth. This is born-again. After burning our old nature, the Spirit of God molds us to resemble the Lord Jesus. This explanation of born-again is the reason why I wrote this book.

Any other explanation outside this one given us by the Lord Jesus is from Satan and his agents. I am sure you don't want any further explanation about "believe" or born-again except you are still confused. If this is your case, let me come down more for you to understand this very well.

The Lord Jesus is saying that the person seeking for the new-birth does not have to search for it in books, through works, through self-righteousness or from anywhere, but from the "Words" from His mouth. This is not a parable, but a straightforward message.

No one can command the Holy Spirit of God to come and give you the second birth. The Pope cannot do it, neither any modern-day apostle nor prophet. We need no placing on of hands from anyone in order to receive the spirit birth.

We need no lengthy prayers to exhaust our strength. We need no quack pastor to charm us to fall down. It's the words that proceed out from the mouth of the Lord Jesus that we must read, listen and observe in order to receive the Spirit-birth.

Therefore, any pastor, apostle, bishop, or evangelist who prays for you to receive the Holy Spirit of God is a liar from the devil who has not the Word of God in him. Whatever these imposters tell you about born-again is deceptive.

Let me take you to a renowned televangelist called Billy Graham who is known to be the most popular televangelist who organized over four hundred crusades and evangelized to over two hundred million people during his lifelong ministry.

I watched his preaching on YouTube entitled "Billy Graham, Ye Must be Born-Again." After watching the video, no one would tell you that Billy Graham was not born-again. At the end of the preaching, he invited those who wanted to receive Christ to get up from their seats and come forward to the stage.

Thinking he will ask them to search the portions of the Bible that gives us words that comes directly from the mouth of the Lord Jesus and those that comes from the apostles, he prayed for them to receive the spirit-birth.

Is this born-again? How could Billy Graham give people the spirit-birth when he didn't have it himself? Billy Graham passed away in February 2018 without being born again.

He, together with his followers who have also passed away are now awaiting the final judgment in tumultuous chambers in eternity. If you are one of his followers or fans, you must draw back early before it is too late.

At this point, I would like the apostle Peter, to add his voice to what His master, has said about how to become born-again:

> "Being born again, not of corruptible seed, but of incorruptible, by the word of God, which liveth and abideth for ever."
>
> 1 Peter 1: 23.

The apostle has also mentioned that we can never become born-again by corruptible seeds. The corruptible seeds include the chanting of Jesus' name like what I did at that local Church in Ghana. This and many other practices, apart from studying the words, which proceeds out of the mouth of the Lord Jesus, are "corruptible seeds."

The lengthy prayers, sacrifices, sprinkling of water, burning of incense and candles, counting of rosary and practicing of righteous life cannot give you the Spirit-birth. Regular Church attendances, paying of tithe, giving of big offering, fasting and recital of Psalms can also not give you the new-birth.

The Word of God has spoken and is asking you to desist from "corruptible seeds." It is good to obey by throwing away what these cult Churches and pastors have taught you. They are all liars who are pushing you from the truth of God to the lies of Satan. The Word of God is the only truth that we must believe to live:

> "God forbid: yea, let God be true, but every man a liar."
>
> Romans 3: 4.

As one continues to learn and observe every Word that comes out from the Mouth of the Lord Jesus, the spiritual birth takes place. The process is accelerated through regular studying of the Words from the mouth of the Lord Jesus not the entire Bible or the New Testament.

I am not saying here that you should stop reading the Old Testament or the New Testament. You could read the entire Bible to know more about God and his dealings with humanity. This is a good thing to do, but concerning the spirit-birth, you must only read the words that comes out from the mouth of the Lord and observe them.

A new Christian convert is a baby in Christianity likewise any long serving Christian who does not know the Words from the mouth of the Lord Jesus. You can know the Words from the mouth of the Lord Jesus by constantly reading the New Testament. The Holy Spirit talks to us about this:

> "Wherefore laying aside all malice, and all guile, and hypocrisies, and envies, and all evil speakings, As newborn babes, desire the sincere milk of the word, that ye may grow thereby."
>
> 1 Peter 1:2.

As a new Christian seeking to become born-again, the scripture above is telling you to endeavor to put away the following:

- ❖ "Malice" i.e. hatred.
- ❖ "All guile" i.e. claiming as if you were wiser than all people, or when you use cunning means to cheat others.
- ❖ "Hypocrisies" i.e. claiming you have higher standards or beliefs in religion or in Christianity more than others do when in fact it's not true.
- ❖ "Envies" i.e. being discontented with what you have and wishing what others have were yours.
- ❖ "And all evil speakings." This is adulterating the scripture, and speaking evil words against the Word of God or blaspheming the Holy Trinity. It also includes using filthy words.

The Comforter gave the above scripture (testament, commandment, or instruction) to the apostle Peter, and for that matter, it forms part of the words from the mouth of the Lord Jesus. Therefore, the instruction is for every new convert or Christian seeking for the new-birth.

Instructions of this kind, and in fact every word from the mouth of the Lord Jesus is what the Bible refers to as the "sincere milk of the Word." This is what both new Christian converts and old Christians need every day in order to grow.

Indeed, the Word from Jesus' mouth and those from Jesus' apostle are what we must read, and listen to. This is what the Lord Jesus refers to as "Believe." This is what everyone who claims to be Christian need every day until the person has become born-again.

19

THE WORDS FROM JESUS' MOUTH IS SPIRITUAL FOOD

The message from the mouth of the Lord Jesus is what every Christian need to become born-again. This is what we call the "Word" of God. However, pastor imposters; have misconstrued the "Word" of God with reading of the entire Bible. The syndrome is everywhere these last days.

The Lord Jesus is the Word of God. He's also called the "Bread of life," or "The Bread from Heaven." Bread is the most common food everywhere in the world. Virtually, every race eat bread as food.

When the Bible says the Lord Jesus is Bread from Heaven. It wants to tell Christians that we must eat the Words from the mouth of the Lord Jesus the same way as we eat bread. The moment a Christian eats this bread (words from Jesus' mouth) he or she gets eternal life.

Prior to forwarding the manuscript of this book for publishing, the last sermon preached in the Church, I visited that Sunday was on the theme: "The Bread of Life." The Bible verse was taken from the book of John:

> "I am the living bread which came down from heaven: if any man eat of this bread, he shall live for ever: and the bread that I will give is my flesh, which I will give for the life of the world."
>
> John 6: 51.

I know what exactly the bread, which came down from Heaven, is so I was happy to meet the topic on this fateful Sunday. When the pastor started, I could see him trying his best to make good points out of the scripture quote, but much as he tried the farther away, he got from the truth.

I found the pastor talking about the Lord Jesus all right, but he refused to concentrate on what actually is the bread. I saw that he was always concentrating on the good things the Lord Jesus can offer all those who come to him.

The rightful statement I ever heard him repeating all the time was, 'You must take Jesus as your personal savior.' After saying this, he will add, 'Because he is the son of God who is ready to help us with all our needs and can grant us eternal life."

Sometimes, he will ask, 'have you taken Jesus as your personal savior.' The statement is true, but I saw a great deviation and a big sign of ignorance on the side of a well-trained pastor of his caliber.

I felt sorry for the preacher and didn't take any interest in whatever he was saying. I was only happy to have been in the Church room that fateful Sunday which is the Lord's Day, because I have got a serious point to add to this book.

The Words from the mouth of the Lord Jesus is spiritual food. So the Lord Jesus is "the bread from Heaven," meaning that the Lord Jesus has certain information from his mouth which every Christian must seek to eat. The Lord says, "if any man eat of this bread, he shall live for ever."

The Lord Jesus told us; "The words that I speak unto you, they are spirit, and they are fire." Now He's telling us that He is the bread from Heaven. If He's bread, then we must eat Him; and the only way to do this is to eat (read) and observe the Words that comes out from His mouth.

If you don't eat food, you shall die. In the same way, if you don't eat (read and observe) the Lord Jesus (the words from his mouth) you shall spiritually die. This also means that if you compile the words from his mouth and begin to live according to them, you will become born-gain to inherit eternal life.

The Lord concludes that "And the bread that I will give is my flesh, which I will give for the life of the world." The Lord Jesus says the bread (Word) from his mouth is his flesh. This means that He descended from Heaven purposely to deliver some specific words to humanity.

This implies that the moment you begin to study and practice the words from the mouth of the Lord Jesus you eat his flesh. Anybody in the world who shall eat this meat receives the new-birth. The Lord Jesus again hinted us about this secret during His encounter with Satan:

> "Man shall not live by bread alone, but by every word that proceedeth out of the mouth of God."

> Matthew 4: 4.

As I mentioned earlier, we eat food to grow physically, but we eat the Words from the mouth of the Lord Jesus to receive the Spirit-birth and to grow spiritually. With this backdrop the common question; "Have you taken Jesus as your personal savior" becomes null and void.

By asking this question, do the preacher want you to carry Jesus on your back, or carry Him in your bags like how the Jehovah witness carry their Jehovah in hand bags? This is not the correct way to eat the flesh of the Lord Jesus.

If therefore a preacher preaches the whole day as if he were an angel, but did not give you instructions from the mouth of the Lord Jesus that can help you to grow in Him, my good friend, forget the preacher.

Tell all those fond of preaching sermons about the life of Jesus and the miracles He did to stop wasting your precious time. On the contrary, appraise and give sound ears to preachers who give you systematic instructions from the mouth of the Lord Jesus and His apostles.

20

THE WORD OF GOD IS THE SWORD OF THE SPIRIT

From our studies in the previous chapter, the Words from the mouth of the Lord Jesus is his body. Therefore, if you continue to study these words, your body changes into spiritual body of the Lord Jesus. Such a body turns into sword against all perils. The Word of God hinted us:

> "And take the helmet of salvation, and the sword of the Spirit, which is the word of God."
>
> Ephesians 6:17.

The command is for every Christian to take "the helmet of salvation." This is to have faith. The second command is to take "the sword of the spirit," which is the words from the mouth of the Lord Jesus. After this, you get "the sword of the spirit" in your hand.

Therefore, if you want to conquer idols, wizards, witchcraft or any power of the devil, you need to have faith and study the Word of

God. You don't have to go to all-night or take any directives from any sham man of God to sacrifice doves, fowls and the rest.

You don't need sticker or calendar from these quack ministers, false apostles and false prophets. You don't have to buy any holi water or holi oil in order to get this sword of the spirt. You don't need prayers or fasting either.

The word of God has not instructed you to do so. What you must do is to study the words from the mouth of the Lord Jesus. When you receive the spirit-birth, the spirit leads you wherever you go and in anything, you do. The Lord Jesus also comes to dwell in you, which automatically makes you "the son of God":

> "For as many as are led by the Spirit of God, they are the sons of God."
>
> Romans 8: 14.

Note very well that when the spirit enters into you, you no longer live for yourself, but for the Lord Jesus. When the Spirit enters into you, you get your own independent spirit from the Lord, which protects you every time. The Bible tells us about the Spirit in us after we have become born-again:

> "For ye have not received the spirit of bondage again to fear; but ye have received the Spirit of adoption, whereby we cry, Abba, Father. The Spirit itself beareth witness with our spirit, that we are the children of God."
>
> Romans 8:15–16.

I have observed that thousands of Christians who rush to faith-healers and modern televangelists like Pastor Chris, T. B. Joshua, Joseph Duplantis, Joyce Meyers, Joel Oesten, and countless others are panicked with fear of failure in life.

They also fear idols, witchcrafts, wizards and evil people in their communities. Instead of going to the Lord Jesus by reading His words for the sword of the spirit, they turn to these sham men of God who initiate them into Satanic worship without their knowing.

So many Christians worship with Churches that have descent teaching and Bible lessons. Their order of worship, Church organization, and Christian ethics looks descent and enchanting. This has attracted the middle class and scholars into their Churches.

Once these Churches do not preach the Words from the mouth of the Lord Jesus, you must avoid attending these Churches. The reason is that these Churches are part of the Ecumenical Movement spearheaded by the Pontiff of Rome that is leading all men into the one-world religion.

Over here, in the Ecumenical Movement, you are given temporal relieve of your problems by these sham men of God through the powers of familiar spirits. As the first problem begins to dwindle, Satan pushes another one to you.

Satan continues to push different problems to you to prevent you from breaking the relationship between you and that particular sham man of God and his Church. This is the reason why you see so many people remain stuck with some of these devil Churches.

At times, you may see so many members in one particular Church. Most of these people may be witches and wizards. Others may be black magicians and evil occultist who may need rest from their torments.

These tormentors may be group of witchcraft or wizards whose society the person might have joined. For example, one may bring his or her child for religious sacrifice. When it comes to the turn of some of them, they will refuse to donate.

This turns into a serious spiritual scuffle, and the only people who are able to solve these spiritual problems are the sham men of God, faith healers, thousands of televangelists, and self-acclaimed bishops, prophets, apostles, angels and pastors. They take their defense in these sham men of God.

The one born of the Spirit takes his defense in the Spirit. The Bible tells us about this defense in the Lord God after we have become His sons:

> "If God be for us, who can be against us?"
>
> Romans 8: 31.

The Word of God is telling us that we are hundred percent protected in the Lord God as soon as we become born-again. What is the need to fear a witchcraft, an idolater, an evil co-worker, a wicked proprietor or the one who hates you because of the love you have for the Lord?

Wait as the Lord Jesus tells you more about taking the sword of the spirit:

> "Jesus answered and said unto him, If a man love me, he will keep my words: and my Father will love him, and we will come unto him, and make our abode with him."
>
> John 14: 23.

Imagine a situation where the Lord God and the Lord Jesus has made their dwelling place in you. What shall you lack and who can conquer you? The moment you ask, it is granted unto you. Anytime the enemy attacks, his bullets fall on solid iron.

When the Lord God and the Lord Jesus have built their house in you, they will stock the house with food, drinks and every basic need. They will pay for utility bills in advance and guide the house 24/7. All you will do is to sleep peaceful in this house:

21

THE BORN-AGAIN PERSON HAS EVERYTHING HE NEEDS

The Lord God again promises us:

> "He that spared not his own Son, but delivered him up for us all, how shall he not with him also freely give us all things?"
>
> Romans 8: 32.

The above Scripture quote is telling every born-again Christian to ask the Lord for everything they need. If we have such a big opportunity opened to us, why do some of us rush to places where the Lord has not asked us to go?

Why should you ask a pastor to do something for you when the Lord himself is telling you to believe every word from his mouth so that you can get whatever you want. This makes you a disobedient Christian who doesn't respect your Lord and your God.

The Lord Jesus says we should cast our burdens upon him. He didn't tell us to cast our burdens upon T.B. Joshua, Pastor Chris, T.D. Jakes, Joseph Duplantis, or Duncan Williams. He didn't tell us to cast our burdens upon Mensah Otabil, Joyce Meyers or any of the renowned tele-evangelists you see on TV screens today.

None of them has the authority to solve your problems. They are equally accountable to the Lord Jesus as you. It's only the Lord Jesus who invites us to come to him with our problems for him to solve them for us. We are accountable to Him alone.

From today, note very well that God is not a respecter of man who would be forced to respect those who doesn't obey His beloved Jesus Christ. Therefore, if your problem is sickness, poverty, unemployment, etc., all you need to do is to carry them to the Lord Jesus in prayers for possible solutions.

Before you do, try as much as you can to begin observing the words that comes from the mouth of the Lord Jesus. Even if you promise the Lord Jesus that you'll from this day manage to observe the Words from His mouth, this alone would be enough to grant the solutions to your problems.

When the Lord sees that you respect his commandments, He respects you back by admitting you into His bosom. He gives you rest and the burdens you carry are taken away.

The Lord Jesus says; "YE MUST BE BORN AGAIN." On our path to receiving the second birth, we must be patient with Him if our prayer requests don't come on time. He knows you by name, by residence, by whatever you need and when you need this.

Slow response to our prayer requests has compelled most of us to rush to places where we are not supposed to go. This retards our progress to receiving the new-birth. Whether you're born-again or not, there is one thing you must know.

The Lord God has reserved quick response to our prayers until the time of the Kingdom of God.

Read Isaiah Chapter 65. Space would not allow me to explain this Bible quote in full. All I can say is that, once we are humans, we may lack certain things, and some of our prayer requests may delay.

However, we shall see this no more when we joyfully enter into the Kingdom of God. Notwithstanding, the Lord is always ready to help us:

> "But my God shall supply all your need according to his riches in glory by Christ Jesus."
>
> Philippians 4: 19.

If God is able to supply Christians with all our needs, then we must reason as humans never to attend all-night services and prayer sessions organized by sham men of God. When you pray as a Christian, you must patiently wait for the answer.

When your request is not coming as quick as you want, continue to exercise self-restraint. The Lord knows the right time you need what you have requested from him. I will not conclude this short lesson without chipping in one important commandment of the Lord.

In this commandment, the Lord Jesus is telling you and me to do something, which most of us know already, but have ignored. If your prayer request is not getting the right response from the Lord, it might be due to your neglect of this important commandment:

> "But seek ye first the kingdom of God, and his righteousness; and all these things shall be added unto you."
>
> Matthew 6: 33.

According to this commandment, if we want to receive "all things" that we ask in prayers or desire in this life, we must do something. This is to "seek ye first the Kingdom of God and his righteousness."

We know that we receive the Kingdom of God only by believing in the Lord Jesus and becoming spiritually born-again. We can know His righteousness only after studying the Words from the mouth of the Lord Jesus and the Bible.

Having landed this way let me give you two most important things every Christian needs in this life and in the next to come. According to the Lord Jesus, we must "believe" in Him in order to become born-again. This will grant us the opportunity to enter into the Kingdom of God.

Again, He tells you to seek for the Kingdom of God and His righteousness and all other things shall be added unto you including all the material things you need in life. Regarding all things, this is what He again tells us:

> "Take therefore no thought for the morrow: for the morrow shall take thought for the things of itself. Sufficient unto the day is the evil thereof."
>
> Matthew 6:33–34.

"Take therefore no thought for the morrow" means, we shouldn't burden ourselves with so many wants in the next day or future times. The reason is that tomorrow is not for us. We can't tell whether we shall live or die. We should rather concentrate on knowing the mysteries of the Kingdom of God and His righteousness.

The Lord continues that "For the morrow shall take thought for the things of itself." Meaning that whether it shall rain or shine on your life, this will depend upon the Lord Jesus.

Finally, the Lord says, "Sufficient unto the day is the evil thereof." This means that so many people have fallen from grace to condemnation for following earthly things. What can you say to this? All I can say is that let every little thing you have become sufficient unto you with thanksgiving unto the Lord.

22

HOW TO KNOW YOU ARE BORN OF THE SPIRIT

I have already given you details on how to receive the spirit-birth and to become born-again. What remains is knowing whether you are born-again or not. It is necessary to know this so that you can draw a distinct line between the born-again person and the one who is not.

The promise about the new-birth (born-again) which the Lord Jesus decreed upon his disciples came in the days of Ezekiel when the Lord God hinted the world:

> "Then will I sprinkle clean water upon you, and ye shall be clean: from all your filthiness, and from all your idols, will I cleanse you."
>
> Ezekiel 36; 25.

Over here, the Lord God was talking about the water and Spirit baptism, which He said we shall need in order to become born-again. Long before the Lord Jesus came to introduce the Water and Spirit baptism, the Lord God had foretold us about the changes the person who receives the Holy Spirit shall go through.

> "A new heart also will I give you, and a new spirit will I put within you: and I will take away the stony heart out of your flesh, and I will give you an heart of flesh."
>
> Ezekiel 36; 26

This implies that after receiving the Spirit baptism, the Christian believer no longer remains the same. The Lord puts a new spirit and a new heart within you. From this time, the Spirit of God control and guides you every minute of your life. The Lord told us through the prophet Isaiah:

> "And I will put my spirit within you, and cause you to walk in my statutes, and ye shall keep my judgments, and do them."
>
> Ezekiel 36: 27.

After one is born-again, the person can feel the spirit of God within the body, which enables him to discern between what, is good and what is evil. The spirit therefore helps us to abstain from evil.

Everything the unbeliever does becomes abominable unto you.

Fornication, drunkenness, stealing, idolatry and all sorts of evil and wickedness, becomes a scorn to you. The new heart, which is the new spirit given you by the Lord moves you to love the Lord God, the Lord Jesus, and the Holy Spirit.

The Spirit again helps you to understand the Bible perfectly well and pushes you to love your neighbor as yourself, particularly, to have pity on needy persons. At this time, the Christian's lifestyle changes and his or her delight in worldly things become subsided.

This is the time the Lord God and the Lord Jesus come down to you and make their dwelling in you. This is a wonderful revelation that every Christian must take very serious.

After learning and observing the Words that proceed out from the mouth of the Lord Jesus, you must know your stance in Him:

> "Examine yourselves, whether ye be in the faith; prove your own selves. Know ye not your own selves, how that Jesus Christ is in you, except ye be reprobates?"
>
> 2 Corinthians 13: 5.

The Lord Jesus is in us except that there are certain things we do in secret that the commandments of the Lord prevents us from doing. If you live according to the words from the mouth of the Lord, then I tell you, the Lord Jesus Christ is in you.

Once He's in you, there is no need to entertain sham men of God who behave as if they were people who have the true Lord Jesus or the Holy Spirit in them. Some of them frighten people as if they have some supernatural influence over everybody; and that they are super-humans.

Obinin of Ghana is one of them. Reverend *Obofo* is another. T. B. Joshua, Kum Chacha, and countless other televangelist and self-acclaimed mushroom men of God around the globe are also part of the swindle.

You call these pastors instead of posters; prophets instead of puppets; apostles instead of apostates; and angels instead of anglers. Most of them frighten you with words and behave as if they have the power of God. They may have powers, but this is not the true power of God.

The Word of God promises sincere Christians that we shall change at the time of the Lord Jesus' second coming. In this change, we expect to see new indelible bodies with new spirits given to all sincere believers at the same time.

Until this change occurs in the near future, any man or woman who stands in a Church room during ministration, prayers or healing time and shaking as if he or she's superior in spirit to every Christian uses familiar spirit and is a devil. He or she might also be lunatic.

When the spirit indwells a person, it causes him to be sober, respectful; calm and gentle. You become afraid to sin because the Lord Jesus who is in you will call your attention to whatever sin you are about to commit.

When the Spirit of God is in you, it doesn't mean you should speak in tongues, prophesy, perform miracles, and heal people or do any extra-ordinary spiritual work. Getting any of these gifts depends upon the discretion of the Lord Jesus.

Notwithstanding, now that the New Testament has been given us, what do we need signs and wonders, prophecies and tongues for. Search the scriptures thoroughly and you will know that no signs and wonders can occur again after the Pentecostal experience and the Acts of the Apostles.

The Bible makes it clear that the next signs and wonders shall occur at the Lord Jesus' second coming. If you extend your search deeper, the Bible will tell you the specific type of signs and wonders we must expect at that time.

Sincere Christian believers need no prophecies either. Everything we want to know is recorded in the Bible for us. The lies and useless predictions which Christian quacks and charlatans give you are not prophecies, but imaginative lies from their own hearts. The Lord warns us to keep away from them:

> "Thus saith the LORD of hosts, Hearken not unto the words of the prophets that prophesy unto you: they make you vain: they speak a vision of their own heart, and not out of the mouth of the LORD."
>
> Jeremiah 23: 16.

In spite of this, the Lord God does so many wonders these last days. He heals the seriously sick, save people from danger, protect most of us from our enemies and open up chances for His beloved ones.

The Lord grants his children's prayer request in a special way beyond our imagination. The Lord also deliver us from accidents, and strange situations which otherwise might have endangered our lives. I am talking about this miracle.

I do not mean the magic that goes on in Church rooms, but what sincere Christians experience in their private lives. Besides this, the Lord reveals Himself to people to let them know that He exists. Through such happenstances, many people had believed the Lord Jesus and had become born-again Christians.

I am a beneficiary of such astonishing revelations by the Lord Jesus, which converted me to become a Christian. Therefore, I can never deny the miraculous works which the Lord do for his children these last days. The Lord lives and shall continue to live forever. Thank you Lord Jesus.

Much as the Lord reveals himself today and performs wonders in people's lives. I cannot confirm the truthfulness in the concert of tele-evangelists claiming to perform signs and wonders on Television screens.

When the Spirit of God is in you, your prayer is always different from the heathen and lukewarm Christians who have not the Spirit. First, every prayer you make to the Lord is full of thanksgiving and praises.

Secondly, during prayers, the Spirit directs you to pray for the coming of the Kingdom of God. This fulfills the believer's obligation, which is one of the commandment by the Lord to set our affections on things above and pray for the coming of the Kingdom of God.

I cannot leave this topic without touching on one most important point. In my experience as a Christian, I have never dreamt about the Kingdom of Heaven and seen God or Jesus before. Likewise, I don't think it's necessity for me or any other born-again Christian to have such dreams before we can attest to the fact that the Lord God is alive.

In my discernment, I have found all those who claim to have dreamt about the Kingdom of Heaven to be blatant liars. Most of them claim they have seen angels, Jesus, the Saints of the Lord, God or hellfire. They are all fake dreamers.

As for hellfire, I believe whatever they say about it because it is the home of their master-Satan, but the rest of their dreams are imaginative stories.

I will never believe them, and I will urge you not to believe them neither today nor tomorrow. The reason is that all their narratives and description of this majestic city of God and the Godhead have always been in variance with the true description of what is recorded in the Bible.

To be spirit-filled is truly an interesting and a wonderful experience. Any sentence of the Bible you read is explained to you. This makes you live as if the Lord Jesus stands before you everyday. You find great delight in Him, and have pity for humankind all the time.

The book of Romans adds a little to the Christian experience with the Spirit-birth:

> "And if Christ be in you, the body is dead because of sin; but the Spirit is life because of righteousness. But if the Spirit of him that raised up Jesus from the dead dwell in you, he that raised up Christ from the dead shall also quicken your mortal bodies by his Spirit that dwelleth in you."
>
> Romans 8:10–11.

You see that the Spirit of the Lord is always with the born-again child of God and I bet you, this person will not succumb to useless and vain preaching, prayers, and miracles, neither will the person respect anyone who deliberately shakes himself at the time of prayers as if he were filled with the Spirit of God.

This is how God's Holy Spirit works with true Christian believers today. God's Holy Spirit cannot be commanded to operate as we see in Church rooms. He cannot be invited by any prophet, bishop or apostle to appear on stage.

The spirit that moves people to shiver, scream, roll on the floor, is familiar spirits, not the Spirit of God. This raises the point whether the miracles, signs and wonders we see today on TV screens are genuine. To know the truth, I will recommend to you my soon coming book entitled:

Signs and Wonders: is it for Today?

23

YOU HAVE NO EXCUSE

If you have followed this book up to this point, I will urge you to complete the rest because there are so many revelations, which can help you to become born-again. If you are already born-again, you also need this vital information to enable you to grow in the Spirit until you have received another important power of God called "Faith."

You might also be someone who is wavering in mind about the Lord Jesus and Christianity because of what quack ministers of God are doing these last days. You must continue reading this book because this is the time to know who the Lord Jesus is and why you must not delay to give your life to him.

I have approached so many pastors who do not know exactly what born-again is. Most of them are true Christians seeking for the truth and desirous to enter into the Kingdom of God, but the Bible colleges they attended brainwashed them until they know nothing about this all-important concept.

Brainwashing is a serious incurable disease, which takes time to heal. If you are one of them, you must also take the time to complete reading this book. It's all about your single soul, and your entry into the Kingdom of God.

If this is really, your goal on earth you must agree to the fact that all human beings were born into sin. The Word of God boldly tells us:

> All we like sheep have gone astray; we have turned everyone to his own way; and the LORD hath laid on him the iniquity of us all."

Isaiah 53: 6.

It is a fact that everybody has turned his own way doing what pleases us these last days. I know a popular Church in Accra that teaches that we are the salt of the world. Because of that, the leader uses salt for the administration and control of his Church.

Members of this Church fast and pray with salt. They heal their wounds with salt and sprinkle salt in their compounds, rooms, offices and cars. What is the meaning of all these? The members have become blind followers doing everything this foolish founder asks them to do.

You blind followers! Why not use bread rather, because the Lord Jesus says He's the bread of life. Is bread not worth more than salt? Better still, why are these Church members not eating and drinking salt for food and beverage? Sometimes I wonder how people read and interpret the Bible.

Today, So many Churches are using oil which they call "anointing oil" to cure and for the performance of wonders. Their members purchase the oil and use them to fast and pray for prosperity and protection. They do this and still call themselves Christians.

Sad enough, the oil they use is the best edible oil, which in fact performs no signs or wonders for them. If oil could perform wonders, why not use to fry meat and rather use the meat because fried meat is more valuable than when the oil stands alone.

This is not all. Since the early twenties, the use of stickers has become phenomenal with some Churches bringing into ridicule the Christian worship. These stickers have the pictures of these foolish pastors and sham men of God on them.

It is sad to see scholars and respectable people using these useless stickers side-by-side with the poor and illiterate folks. Some members paste these useless stickers on their cars, rooms, stalls and pockets for spiritual protection, prosperity in business and long life. Is this not Spiritism?

At what time did, the Lord Jesus transferred his powers into dumb images which performs no wonders. There are so many Churches out there that use fan, handkerchiefs, pots, calendar, and different items that I can't mention here to worship, but who are you to tell their members that they are at the wrong place. They will call you "the devil."

I went to the shop of a young woman and found the sticker of the so-called self-acclaimed man of God in Ghana called Reverend *Obofo* meaning angel. After paying her, she opened her drawer to give me a change. I then saw the sticker and asked her to throw it away because it contained nothing from the Lord Jesus.

The lady, instead of replying yes or no, told me; 'If you continue to challenge the sticker of *Obofo* this way, you could become mad.' What a funny comment! I wondered why the woman didn't ask me why I said so, but instead attacked me. She had invested all her trust in this sticker.

Why should you leave behind the Love of the Lord Jesus and follow religious quacks and charlatans? Once again, I want to draw your attention to this important scripture from the book of John:

> "Jesus answered and said unto him, If a man love me, he will keep my words: and my Father will love him, and we will come unto him, and make our abode with him."
>
> John 14: 23.

Where are you my dear reader, and how do, you understand this Bible text. The Lord Jesus you claim to worship is telling you to observe every word that proceeds out from his mouth. If you respect Him, you will obey this simple instruction.

According to him, as soon as you do this, He will give a good report about you to the Lord God Almighty. This shall be followed by the two of them coming to build their houses in your body. Is this not an amazing promise?

He commanded us in the book of John; "If ye love me, keep my commandments." John 14:15. According to the Lord Jesus, the moment we keep His commandments, He does something for us. Let's have a look at this particular thing:

> "And I will pray the Father, and he shall give you another Comforter, that he may abide with you for ever; Even the Spirit of truth; whom the world cannot receive, because it seeth him not, neither knoweth him: but ye know him; for he dwelleth with you, and shall be in you."
>
> John 14:16–17.

According to the above scripture, the moment we keep the commandments of the Lord Jesus, He sends the Comforter to come and dwell in us. Therefore, after keeping the commandments of the Lord, something strange happens to you the Christian.

The Almighty God, The Lord Jesus and the Comforter, also called the Holy Ghost comes and build their houses in you and dwell with you always. According to the scripture, those in the world doesn't see them, but you see them because they dwell in you.

The scripture above never mentioned the name of any pastor, bishop, prophet, apostle or an angel. He never mentioned prayers, fasting, tithing, anointing oil, holi oil, or any other thing here. The big question now is, has the Lord Jesus transferred the love He says we should have for him into these servile flattery ministers of God?

Has He transferred the love He says we should have in him into these salt, edible oils, handkerchiefs, stickers, toys and implements which these sham men of God use today? Why don't you keep the words of the Lord Jesus so that you can enjoy the Christian benefits to the full?

Magnet attracts magnet, and your regular visit to these sham men of God means that you are evil yourself.

I tell you frankly that once you give yourself to false Christian Churches or visit false men of God and take their prayers, holi water and anointing oils, you are a sinner and the Lord Jesus doesn't know you. I'll prove this to you. In a short Bible lesson taken from the book of 2 Corinthians 4: 3–5.

> 2 Corinthians 4: 3 "But if our gospel be hid, it is hid to them that are lost."

The above scripture is warning every Christian not to hide the gospel truth. If anybody should hide the gospel truth, it should be non-Christians. The secret in this short verse of the Bible is that the moment you over look one key instruction or commandment of the Bible as a Christian, you hide a gospel truth.

Those who hide single Bible facts that they come across when reading the Bible are classified as unbelievers. The Word of God tells us more:

> 2 Corinthians 4: 4 "In whom the god of this world hath blinded the minds of them which believe not, lest the light of the glorious gospel of Christ, who is the image of God, should shine unto them."

My dear reader, the scripture you just read has made it clear that the moment you overlook one commandment of the Lord Jesus or His apostles, you are unbeliever. It continues that for you not taking serious note of the particular instruction or commandment is the work of the gods of this earth.

The gods of this world are the televangelists, the apostate pastors and bishops who doesn't preach the truth of the Bible. They have written several Christian books, but none contains an iota of truth from the gospel.

They operate their private TV and radio stations, and have spread their tentacles throughout the internet and in the print media, but I tell you, they are sham and tainted beyond disgrace before the Almighty God and the Lord Jesus.

They hate you and are pulling most of you to accept the soon coming one-world religion. The lesson continues to tell you why the Lord God abhors them:

> 2 Corinthians 4: 5 "For we preach not ourselves, but Christ Jesus the Lord; and ourselves your servants for Jesus' sake."

According to the scripture text above, the moment a preacher stands to preach, the message should be the message from "Christ Jesus our Lord." Before I continue, can you tell me the message from Christ Jesus our Lord?

I will tell you myself. The message from Christ Jesus our Lord is the message that comes directly from His mouth. If you don't know, I will give you one example.

> "And when thou prayest, thou shalt not be as the hypocrites are: for they love to pray standing in the synagogues and in the corners of the streets, that they may be seen of men. Verily I say unto you, They have their reward. But thou, when thou prayest, enter into

thy closet, and when thou hast shut thy door, pray to thy Father which is in secret; and thy Father which seeth in secret shall reward thee openly."

Matthew 6:5–6

The above scripture is the message from the mouth of the Lord Jesus and this is exactly what the Word of God wants us to preach. Let's have another look at the message from the mouth of Christ Jesus our Lord:

"But when ye pray, use not vain repetitions, as the heathen do: for they think that they shall be heard for their much speaking. Be not ye therefore like unto them: for your Father knoweth what things ye have need of, before ye ask him."

Matthew 6: 7–8.

You see how the message from the mouth of the Lord Jesus is. They are called "Testament of the Lord Jesus," or the "Commandments of the Lord." If you are someone who observes the testament of the Lord Jesus, you will keep the instructions to pray the way He has instructed.

The moment you make repetition in prayers or pray for too long on the same message, thinking you can he heard through that you bleach the Testament of the Lord Jesus and that you don't "believe in the name of the Lord Jesus, and you are not born-again.

If the preacher should ever bring his name into the preaching, it should be to testify to the fact that he or she is nothing as compared to the Lord Jesus. This is the meaning of the scripture we read above which says:

> "For we preach not ourselves, but Christ Jesus the Lord; and ourselves your servants for Jesus' sake."
>
> 2 Corinthians 4:5

What do we see and hear today. A preacher will stand up and tell irrelevant stories about Jesus and His miracles, prosperity and the powers of Jesus. Others will enumerate stories from the Bible and make sweet messages to suit the ears of the congregation.

As the person does this, learned men, women, and respectable people in society would be sitting like dolls clapping hands and giving applauses. Is this not shame on your souls when you cannot pick the Bible and read yourself for the truth.

God hates your pastor, your bishop, your prophet, your apostle and those who claim to be angels because the message in their preaching come from themselves, but not from "Christ Jesus the Lord."

Because these sham men of God don't preach the message from the mouth of "Christ Jesus our Lord," all of you do not believe in Him and you are not born again. The secret name and title of the Lord Jesus that His apostles used for him is CHRIST JESUS THE LORD.

The Word of God has fore-warned us about these sham men of God in the book of Colossians. Let's read from Chapter 2 Verse 20–23.

> Colossians 2: 20 "Wherefore if ye be dead with Christ from the rudiments of the world, why, as though living in the world, are ye subject to ordinances."

This means that if you claim to be Christian, who is baptized in water to signify the death of all you sins; and if you have been baptized in the Spirit to see the mystery of the Kingdom of God, you must avoid something called "rudiments."

Rudiments are cunning words from preachers, false teachings, and traditions of men, the prosperity gospel, and the use of images, toys and forms that Christian Churches are using these days. These have no basis for eternal life.

Imagine a pastor who says; "And Jesus took bread and blessed it, and fed them with five thousand people, and there was a miracle." I am asking you! Jesus took bread and blessed it for five thousand people and so what?

It is good sometimes to factor in some of these messages in your preaching, but how can you do this when you have never taught the hungry souls one commandment of the Lord which they need to "Believe" in the Lord Jesus, which they also need to become born-again.

Consider the founder of the Church, who uses salt as the key object for performing signs and wonders in his Church. Is this what the Lord Jesus asks us to do? Are these not ordinances? If you follow these logs, you are "living in the world," and subjecting yourself to "ordinances."

Because of the danger cult Churches pose to some of you the word of God continues to warn you in the following verse:

> Colossians 2:21 "Touch not; taste not; handle not."

My brothers and sisters. If you are seeking to enter into the Kingdom of God. The word of God is telling you "touch not," meaning you shouldn't visit these Churches. Whoever extends invitation to you to visit them is the agent of the devil who wants to destroy you.

"Taste not," meaning you should not listen to their teachings and accept them. Don't let them confuse you. "Handle not," also meaning do not try them at all or accept to become their member. Don't look at their modern auditorium, temples, or their population and join them.

The word of God continues to tell us why we should not visit their Churches, listen to their teachings, or accept to become their members. This carries us to the next verse:

> Colossians 2: 22 "Which all are to perish with the using; after the commandments and doctrines of men?"

According to the scripture above, all those who follow these Churches shall perish into hellfire, because they follow and practice the commandments and doctrines of men not the commandments and doctrines of the Lord Jesus. The Word of God concludes:

> Colossians 2: 23 "Which things have indeed a show of wisdom in will worship, and humility, and neglecting of the body; not in any honour to the satisfying of the flesh."

According to the above scripture, these things are "will worship." This implies that, the kissing of cross, the counting of rosary, the use of holy waters and holy oils, use of incense and candles, the use of back to sender oils, the use of handkerchiefs and stickers, and hundreds of ordinances are all "will worship."

"Will worship" is the type of traditions, customs and beliefs you and your Church have adopted outside the Bible to worship a god other than the Lord God and the Lord Jesus of the Bible. About ninety nine percent of Christian Churches practice "will worship" these last days.

The scripture also mentioned "humility." This also means that some of the cult Churches practice their Christianity in such a humble and subtle manner that if you are someone who do not read the Bible quiet often, you shall join them.

Anyone who becomes a member of these cult Churches is classified as a sinner. All those who go for prayers, all-night services, holi water, back to sender oil, calendar, etc. is not a sincere Christian. You are part of the heathen and a sinner. Indeed, we have all sinned. The word of God reminds us about this:

> "As it is written, there is none righteous, no, not one."
>
> Romans 3: 10.

> "For all have sinned, and come short of the glory of God."
>
> Romans 3: 23.

The reason for human's sinful nature stems from the fact that our grandparents and great grandparents were all idolaters who did not know the Lord Jesus. Even today, after two thousand years have come and gone, some of us have our parents and family members worshipping these dumb idols.

For our disobedience and ignorance, Satan has also heaped uncountable burdens upon most people compelling them to seek for deliverance. In an attempt to go to the Lord Jesus for solutions, they had met these satanic cult Churches, which increase their burdens and enslave them permanently.

Worshipping gods other than the Lord God himself is what the Lord God, our creator hates. This is the reason why He declares all of us as sinners. The Apostle Paul adds more to why we are all guilty of sins before the Lord God:

> "Wherefore, as by one man sin entered into the world, and death by sin; and so death passed upon all men, for that all have sinned."
>
> Romans 5: 12.

Every sinner is like a condemned prisoner before the Lord. The Apostle Paul reveals the consequences for sin and shows a way out from such condemnation:

> "For the wages of sin is death; but the gift of God is eternal life through Jesus Christ our Lord."
>
> Romans 6: 23.

If someone is a condemned prisoner, he or she has no hope anywhere in this world. The sinful world hates you. It's only the Lord God who pities condemned prisoners because He created all of us. According to the scripture above, eternal life is a gift from God, which saves condemned prisoners.

If somebody has a gift, he gives it to the person who pleases him, but this particular gift is for all condemned sinners who repents of their sins and promise to observe all things that the Lord Jesus commanded His disciples.

If you are one of those who follow these fake Churches, prophets and apostles, the Lord Jesus is calling you to turn your back upon them so that you can get this gift today. The Lord does not discriminate by saying that one's sins are too heavy. This gift covers all types of sins, and is free.

I will never leave you ignorant about the fact that the Lord Jesus is also determined to deal treacherously with those who would not accept this free gift. If you see the truth and still maintains your false beliefs, you're without excuse. The Word of God tells us:

> "In flaming fire taking vengeance on them that know not God, and that obey not the gospel of our Lord Jesus Christ."
>
> 2 Thessalonians1: 8.

As soon as you believe in the Lord Jesus and begin to study the Bible, the Lord searches your heart to see if you have truly repented and prepared to observe all things He commanded his disciples. If you qualify, you become born-again and your name is written in the Book of Life.

On the other hand, "Them that know not God, and that obey not the gospel of our Lord Jesus Christ" are those who are not ready to listen to preaching from the mouth of the Lord Jesus. For that matter, they don't "believe" in the name of the Lord Jesus. According to the scripture above, the Lord shall avenge them in flaming fire.

Every born-again child of God has his name written down in the book of life, and those who are not born-again have not their names in this book. The bulk of these people stand the danger of the flaming fire in hell:

> "And whosoever was not found written in the book of life was cast into the lake of fire.
>
> Revelation 20: 15.

The word of God lists eight groups of sinners whose names are not written in the Lamb's book of life. All these people shall not enter into the Kingdom of God:

> "But the fearful, and unbelieving, and the abominable, and murderers, and sexually immoral, and sorcerers, and idolaters, and all liars, shall have their part in the lake which burns with fire and brimstone: which is the second death."
>
> Revelation 21: 8.

If you do not enter into the Kingdom of God, don't blame the Lord Jesus. You might be guilty of one of the above sins. The first is:-

"The Fearful"

The fearful are people who know that the Lord Jesus came to this world because of sinners. They know him as a savior who invites everybody to come for rest for our heavy burdens. (Matthew 11: 28). Notwithstanding, so many people are afraid to abdicate the witchcraft, idols, and the evil spirits they possess.

They fear that these spirits in them may harm or kill them if they throw them away. Sometimes, they feel these powers operating in them are somewhat more potentate than the Lord God Almighty, and the Lord Jesus whose figurative presence they do not see or feel.

Another batch of Christians who fear are those who are not ready to forgo yearly rituals in their hometowns and families. Although they claim to be Christians, yet they sneak quietly to indulge in practices, which include worshipping and pacification to other gods, which the Lord God Almighty abhors.

The next group of the "fearful" includes Christians who have denied the true power in Christianity and as a result contacted a second power in the form of idols, talisman, juju, etc. They feel that these powers provide protection for their families and businesses.

The next batch of people are those who attend Churches, but have denied their faith in the Lord Jesus. They leave their Churches behind them and hop like frogs from one all-night service to the other, and from one prayer camp to the other. They do this to seek for miracles and to listen to false prophecies about their lives.

Another group called the "Fearful" are rich Christians. The Bible has commanded us to share what we have with the poor so that by so doing, we can save treasure in Heaven. The rich fear to share what they have with the poor, because they do not "Believe" the Lord Jesus and the reward He has promised them in the Kingdom of God.

The last group of fearful are people who do not want to become Christians because of their evil non- Christian families, employment or marriages. Others are thieves, soothsayers or spiritualist who fear to stop their profession for fear they might no longer get money to survive life.

To all these category of "fearful" people, the Lord Jesus commands:

> "And if thy right eye offend thee, pluck it out, and cast it from thee: for it is profitable for thee that one of thy members should perish, and not that thy whole body should be cast into hell."
>
> Matthew 5: 29.

It is a command from the Lord to throw away all witchcraft, idols and other spirits without fearing they can harm you later. According to the Word of God, anyone who refuses to do so shall be condemned in hellfire.

The Word of God has promised a special reward for this group of sinners who repent. This reward is concealed in the book of

Revelation. We read these verses every day, but most of us lack the receptacle to capture the secret.

If you are a born-again Christian and wants to know the type of reward, you will enjoy in the Kingdom of God after repelling the spirt of fear in you, please read my soon coming book entitled:

"What Is My Reward in the Kingdom of God?

"The Unbelieving"

The second evil that shall send people to hellfire is "Unbelieving." These are those who doesn't know the truth about born-again. Because of that, they refuse to believe and to observe every word that comes out from the mouth of the Lord Jesus.

They form part of the group that have sold their souls to the devil for power, wealth and fame. Most of them hail from the secret spiritual societies and are mostly the leaders of Christian cult Churches like the Jehovah witness, Seventh-day Adventist, The Mormons, Catholic, and the rest.

They know the Lord Jesus, but have made Him the object of scorn, condemnation and hatred in their Church rooms. They are the apostate Christians who the Lord says shall lead the "Fallen away" (The one-world religion) in the last days.

The next group of "unbelievers" are people who go to Church, but are not born-again. They are not born-again because they do not understand what it is to "believe" in the Lord Jesus and for that matter are not true Christian believers.

The next group of "unbelievers" are those who have rejected every message from the Bible and shifted unto other religions like Buddhism, Judaism, Islam, Hinduism, etc.

The final group are the heathen who do not worship with any religion and would not go to Church either. The Word of God states categorically that all these people shall perish in hellfire.

"The Abominable Persons"

These are people of the world who invoke spirits of the devil, saints and angels. They also include idol worshipers and people who curse to kill their neighbors and co-workers at the least offence.

They also include those who use holi water, anointing oil, incense, candle, lavender, rosary, etc., as a medium to approach the Lord God. Imagine a Christian who stands up and sprinkle herself with a holi oil given her by a pastor with the hope that it can help her to sell well at the market.

Imagine a man who smears his body with holi oil every day before going to the office for the reason that this oil can protect him from his junior workers who are jealous to take his position. All these people have left the Lord Jesus behind and exerted their hopes in something else.

Others have invested their believe in their pastors and sham men of God who induce them to use bless water, handkerchief, salt, oils, dove, parrots, sheep, fowls, etc. According to the Word of God, all these people have no part in the Kingdom of God.

"The sexually immoral"

This includes pre-marital sex that goes on between boys and girls these last days. It also includes married wives who flirt behind their husbands, and married husbands who flirt behind their wives. Men who sexually abuse their maidservants are also included.

The next group on the list are those practicing gay, lesbian and masturbation. Also included are those who sleep with animals like dogs, goats and sheep. The last group are those interested in pornographic videos and pornographic pamphlets.

The more you take delight in viewing these pornographic movies and pictures, the more likely you can indulge in sexual immoral acts. According to the Word of God, all these people shall enter into hell.

"Murderers"

These people cause abortion. They also include those who kill human beings for ritual purposes; including spirit money. They also include people who engage spiritualist to kill their enemies and people who offend them.

Murderers include people who kill for a hire or kill for leisure or for wickedness sake. According to the Word of God, all of them shall enter into hellfire.

If you place false charge on people that leads to their imprisonment and consequent death, you are part of murderers. If you wrongfully divorce your husband or wife which results in the death of the partner as a result of deep cogitating, you have murdered the person.

If you are driver who takes narcotic drugs and drives carelessly to kill passengers or pedestrians, you are part of the murderers group. All these category of people shall go to hell.

"Sorcerers and Idolaters"

These are people who possess magic powers namely: witchcraft, wizard, black magician, warlock, diviner, occultist, voodooist, enchanter, enchantress, necromancer, and magus,

The rest are medicine men and women, shaman, witch doctors, conjurers, rarethaumaturge, thaumaturgist, theurgist, spellcaster, mage, magian, etc. All these group of people shall be burned in hellfire. According to the Word of God, all these people have no part in the Kingdom of God.

"Liars"

Liars are people who deceive people in Jesus's name. Most of them hail from secret societies, and have sold their souls to the devil for money. These people are bound by these societies to tell lies about the Bible and the Lord Jesus.

All the Churches we see today that do not preach Christ crucified, the resurrection of the dead, the second coming of the Lord Jesus, the coming of the Antichrist, hell and hell fire, judgment day, etc., are all liars.

Some of these liar Churches contract powers from witch doctors and black magicians to perform wonders. They normally use holi water, holi oil, handkerchiefs, salt, doves, birds, stickers, calendars, etc. in their ministration.

Liars include Churches, which publish their own Bibles, like the Jehovah witness and the Seventh-day Adventist changing some key words, which lay emphasis on the "Godhead," and "worshipping" of the Lord Jesus.

I will emphatically state that with the exception of the King James Bible, all other Bible versions you see on the market are adulterated. Don't use them because they have been specially written to deceive sincere Christians.

These liars have multiplied in numbers these last days, and with support from the elite Christian conspirators, have taken absolute control over all media homes. They telecast live pseudo miracles, signs and wonders and distribute false Christian books and literature. All of them shall perish in hellfire.

These are the eight groups of condemned sinners destined for destruction in eternal hellfire. If you find your image among the eight, then I ask you to turn immediately to the Lord Jesus and ask for forgiveness of sin. He is merciful to forgive you all of your sins and give you the new-birth.

He paid the price for all these category of sins with His blood. No one would do this voluntary task. The sitting president of America, Canada or Great Britain would never abdicate his position and come to mosquito-infested jungle Africa to mingle with anglers and commoners with the aim of helping to alleviate poverty?

The Lord Jesus left a Heavenly Crown and came to teach you and me to get the Kingdom of God. He was killed, buried and rose again! This is because of His commitment and the Love He has for humanity. The Apostle Paul filled by the Holy Ghost, the Comforter, summarizes this love in a golden verse:

> "But God commended his love toward us, in that, while we were yet sinners, Christ died for us."
>
> Romans 5: 8.

The Lord Jesus himself told us about this love in his conversation with Nicodemus:

> "For God so loved the world, that he gave his only begotten Son, that whosoever believeth in him should not perish, but have everlasting life."
>
> John 3: 16.

Satan has dominated the whole planet through his human agents who have blinded all people including most of you who claim to be Christians. He has spread crime, violence, injustice, war, diseases, terrorism, and false Churches, which teach false gospel.

The Almighty God being a good father won't sit down for this to continue forever. He has determined in his heart to destroy the whole world and make it anew. With this in mind, He has resolved to maintain all those who believe in the Lord Jesus and make them a nation that would worship Him.

Choose whether you would like to be part of this new race or would continue to be part of this present evil generation that He's coming to destroy. If you decide to come with the Lord Jesus, it will be good for your soul. If you refuse and you are finally dumped into hellfire, don't blame the Lord Jesus.

24

PLAN YOUR ESCAPE FROM PLANET EARTH WITH THE LORD JESUS

Imagine the situation where top scientist from the United Nations detect a great fault line in Africa, which they claim could result in a devastating earthquake that would blow off the entire African continent into the sea.

Imagine you were also living in Africa and the United Nations sent an envoy to inform Africans to prepare for a massive evacuation exercise into a safe place in Europe. I 'm sure many people would go because of the threat of this pending earthquake.

Many would go because of widespread killer mosquito infestations, civil wars, ethnic conflicts, energy crisis, severe droughts, and bushfires. Many will follow because of uncontrolled embezzlement of public funds, severe hunger and abject poverty.

Virtually, everybody shall go when the promise comes that the new place in Europe is filled with nice mansions, happiness, justice and peace. If the earthquake finally occurs as predicted, those who believed this story and registered their names shall be saved, whilst those who disbelieved and stayed behind shall perish.

The world we live in is surely coming to its end in fulfillment of biblical prophecies. The Holy Ghost, through the Apostle Peter, leader of the twelve apostles disclosed:

> "But the day of the Lord will come as a thief in the night; in the which the heavens shall pass away with a great noise, and the elements shall melt with fervent heat, the earth also and the works that are therein shall be burned up."
>
> 2 Peter 3: 10.

Sensing the dangers in the destruction, he cautioned us:

> "Looking for and hasting unto the coming of the day of God, wherein the heavens being on fire shall be dissolved, and the elements shall melt with fervent heat?
>
> 2 Peter 3: 12.

All the mighty buildings, factories, shops, vehicles, ships, air planes, dams, bridges, roads, airports, shops, stadia, auditoriums, beautiful scenes, etc. you see today are going to be destroyed completely.

All the gold in the treasury, precious diamond and jewelry, all paper currencies, together with all wicked people shall be set ablaze. The Holy Spirit wants to know your stance if you actually believe that the destruction of the earth is inevitable.

> "Seeing then that all these things shall be dissolved, what manner of persons ought ye to be in all holy conversation and godliness."
>
> 2 Peter 3: 11.

It is only the wise who'll maneuver to live in all "Holy conversation and godliness." "Holy conversation and godliness" is identical with observing the Words from the mouth of the Lord Jesus. The fool shall sit unconcerned in unholy conversation and ungodliness until the destruction of the earth has dawn on them.

Whether you believe it or not, this world shall be destroyed. This is what the Lord God has determined to do. He doesn't need endorsement by the United Nations or the G-8 countries before He can implement the programs that are very dearly on His heart.

It is dearly to the Lord to destroy everything we see because of uncontrolled wickedness, blasphemy, and disobedience to the Word of God.

He's only waiting patiently until the last soul predestined to be saved is saved before He closes the door to all wickedness and abominations on this earth. I wish this last person could be you who now knows what is born-again.

Remember in retrospect that at each time the Lord God wanted to destroy the world, He gave rescue instructions to His obedient children. During the great flood, He instructed Noah who escaped safely through the ark with his eight family members.

During the exodus, He instructed Moses and gave him an escape plan. During the destruction of Sodom and Gomorrah, he instructed Lot and led him, his wife and two daughters into safety. We are now in the final destruction, and being a gracious father, He has given the whole world an escape plan, which is recorded in the Bible.

This escape plan is to "believe" in the Lord Jesus and become born-again. If you believe this, you believe to your own good. If you disbelieve also, you do so at your own condemnation.

For detailed escape plan in the soon coming rapture of the Church, please, read my books entitled;

- ❖ The Rapture is Coming, and
- ❖ Who is going in the Rapture?

25

MANY PEOPLE WANT TO LINGER THESE LAST DAYS

The world is coming to its end and the Lord Jesus is inviting everyone to take refuge in His "believe." Unfortunately, most of those invited are lingering. We see a good example of this same lingering behavior during the Old Testament times.

When the Lord God wanted to destroy the twin city of Sodom and Gomorrah He descended down to earth with the entire Holy Trinity and informed Lot about the destruction. The Lord asked Lot to inform his in-laws who were then living in the twin city about this destruction.

When Lot sent message to them, they did not believe him. They mocked at him for old age and managed to induce him to accept that destruction of the twin city was improbable. Because of this, when the morning came and the Lord asked Lot to run away for his life, he lingered.

The Lord having pity on him hurled him, his wife, and two daughters far away from the city before He set fire into Sodom and Gomorrah.

(Genesis 19: 15, 16). The Lord God has determined in His heart to destroy the world as he did in Noah and Lot's days. The Bible tells us:

> "The LORD of hosts hath sworn, saying, surely as I have thought, so shall it come to pass; and as I have purposed, so shall it stand."
>
> Isaiah 14:24.

He has made open an escape route where everybody; no matter how big your sins are can pass to escape. The only condition is to "believe" in the name of the Lord Jesus. Why linger like Lot? What, if you aren't hurled by God like him?

The Lord is asking you to believe in him so that He can lift you up into safety to another planet until the destruction of the earth is over. Those of us who already know the truth and have become Christians today were once like you.

Some of us were not even worthy to be accepted, but by the Lord's grace we are all sure of our salvation. The Word of God tells us:

> "This is a faithful saying, and worthy of all acceptation, that Christ Jesus came into the world to save sinners; of whom I am chief."
>
> 1 Timothy 1: 15.

The Lord Jesus did not lay down his life for trillions of dollars or for precious gold and diamonds. He died this painful and shameful death at his own discretion because of the love He had for you and me.

Your parents can never do this for you. The partner you love so much can neither do this. You must stand upon this alone to "believe" the Lord Jesus as your savior. The Bible explains in this perfect way:

> "Forasmuch as ye know that ye were not redeemed with corruptible things, as silver and gold, from your vain conversation received by tradition from your fathers; But By faith in Jesus Christ alone you can be saved."
>
> 1 Peter 1: 18.

If you have believed in the Lord Jesus, then I ask you to call and communicate with him all the time. The Bible says:

> "For whosoever shall call upon the name of the Lord shall be saved."
>
> Romans 10: 13.

The word "whosoever" here means that eternal life is open to everybody on earth despite of the person's socio-economic background, race, nationality, ethnicity, gender or age. It also means the Lord doesn't look at the gravity of your sins.

The word 'whosoever,' has laid a solid foundation for all men. The Word of God hints us:

> "For no other foundation can a man lay than that is laid, which is Jesus Christ."
>
> 1 Corinthians 3: 11.

The type of foundation laid for us is further explained:

> "For ye are all the children of God by faith in Christ Jesus."
>
> Galatians 3: 26.

The Apostle Paul finally tells us that "believe" in Jesus Christ makes one become the born-again son of God. The Lord Jesus says: "Ye must be Born-again". This is a command to everyone born of a woman. We must obey this simple command to become the Children of God so that we can get the free entry visas into the Kingdom of God.

I am sure you have read this book with much understanding and will from today believe in the Lord Jesus Christ deep within your heart. If you affirm this, then you need to promise the Lord Jesus that you will continue to "Believe" in him the rest of your life.

Note very well that "believing" in Jesus' name alone is meaningless without the cross. You must believe that Jesus died, was buried and rose again. This is the gospel of Christ, which you must from this day study. The Apostle Paul explains this better:

> The gospel is the death, burial and resurrection of the Lord Jesus Christ.
>
> 1 Corinthians 15:1–4.

Thank you! Lord Jesus.

26

CONCLUSION

If you have absorbed this lesson on born-again very well, please, repeat this prayer and follow it with your heart, soul and mind:

> Almighty God of creation. I admit that I am a sinner deserving of Hell. I understand that it is because of sinners like me that's why the Lord Jesus came to teach us the way into the Kingdom of God.
>
> I humbly ask you to forgive me of my sins; include me among your children and write my name in the Lamb's book of life.
>
> I promise within my heart that I will live the rest of my life obeying the commandments of the Lord Jesus. I therefore ask your Holy Spirit to lead me the way so that I can remain in your tender care and study your words every day.
>
> Dear Father, I humbly ask you to accept this prayer in the name of the Lord and Savior Jesus Christ, Amen.

You have now filled an application form for eternal life, which is in a form of an entry visa into the Kingdom of God. Just as you were born physically to your parents, so are you going to be spiritually born into the family of God.

Once you begin to study the words in the Bible, which proceeded from the mouth of the Lord Jesus you are on the right way. What remains is to absorb these commandments deeply within your heart, soul and mind.

Once you do this, you shall be on the rightful way to becoming born-again Christian, and your abode in the Kingdom of God is assured. Before I leave you, let the Word of God have a final word with you:

> "There be some that trouble you, and would pervert the gospel of Christ. But though we, or an angel from heaven, preach any other gospel unto you than that which we have preached unto you, let him be accursed. As we said before, so say I now again, If any man preach any other gospel unto you than that ye have received, let him be accursed."
>
> Galatians 1:7–9.

I finally ask you to find a Christian Church to attend where the gospel of Christ is preached. If you obey this simple instruction, we shall meet, if not here on earth, it shall be in the rapture spaceship.

In the rapture spacecraft, ask for Ben Amen,

The Slave of the Lord Jesus

Bye for now.

www.ingramcontent.com/pod-product-compliance
Lightning Source LLC
Chambersburg PA
CBHW071656090426
42738CB00009B/1544